MIXED-MEDIA
self-portraits

INSPIRATION & TECHNIQUES

CATE COULACOS PRATO

INTERWEAVE.
interweavebooks.com

2008

EDITOR **Darlene D'Agostino**
ART DIRECTOR / DESIGNER **Karla Baker**
PHOTOGRAPHER **Larry Stein**

Interweave Press LLC
201 East Fourth Street
Loveland, CO 80537-5655 USA
interweavebooks.com

Printed in China by Asia Pacific Offset.

Library of Congress Cataloging-in-Publication Data

Prato, Cate Coulacos.

Mixed media self portraits : inspiration and techniques / Cate Coulacos

Prato, author.
    p. cm.

Includes bibliographical references and index.

ISBN 978-1-59668-082-1 (pbk.)

1. Handicraft. 2. Mixed media. 3. Self-portraits. I.
Title.

TT157.P737 2008

745.5--dc22

2008008682

10 9 8 7 6 5 4 3 2 1

TO MY DAUGHTERS, OLIVIA AND MEREDITH:

"To thine own self be true."

acknowledgments

First and foremost, I have to thank the artists who bared their souls for these self-portrait projects. Clearly, without their talent, hard work, and enthusiasm, this book would not have happened.

I would also like to thank my editors, Tricia Waddell and Darlene D'Agostino, for their guidance and spirit of cooperation. And thanks to the incomparable Larry Stein, for his photography, advice, and willingness to meet me mornings at the Dairy. My coworkers at *Quilting Arts Magazine* and *Cloth Paper Scissors* also deserve my gratitude for putting up with talk about "the book" for months.

I owe a special thanks to Patricia and John Bolton, who not only encouraged me to do this book, but make it a pleasure and a privilege to come to work every day.

And finally, to my husband, Nick: for his appreciation of my work, for all he does to help it happen, and mostly because he has always accepted me as I am and always encouraged me to be my best self.

Trying

to

Age

Grace

so beautiful—loving her at once

Words st...
Crack and so...
break, under th...
Under the tension,
slide, perish,
Decay with imprecision,
will not stay in place,
Will not stay still.
Shrieking voices, or
Scolding, mocking, or
merely chattering,
Always assail them.

14"w × 14"h × 5"d (36 × 36 × 13 cm)
Altered typewriter with found objects

> **self-por·trait** — NOUN: A pictorial or literary portrait of oneself, created by oneself.
> —The American Heritage Dictionary

I know what you're thinking.

Make a self-portrait? Me? Scrutinize myself in the mirror? Face all of my flaws and then try to re-create them in paint, or collage, or fabric?

Relax. Nearly every artist who was invited to contribute to this book had the same reaction. Then, after accepting enthusiastically and saying what a great idea they thought it was, they asked, "Does the self-portrait have to be of me?"

Well, yes. That would be implicit in the term self-portrait.

But I knew what they meant, especially as most of the artists who reacted this way were female. They meant, "Do I have to show my face? My body? Can the artwork portray the inner me, instead? Can I reveal myself in some way other than a physical representation?"

As you will see, all of the artists who participated faced the mirror—or looked deep within—and reflected back amazing works of art in a variety of media. Not only did they lay their souls bare—they actually wrote about it. Some were playful, some introspective, but all were true to themselves.

Working in mixed media will free you to express yourself in unusual, unrepresentational ways. We first saw how much fun—or poignant, or beautiful—this could be in the summer 2005 issue of *Quilting Arts Magazine*. Yvonne Porcella wrote an article on the topic of creative self-portraits done as mini-quilts (similar to the one she created for this book on page 67), and this inspired a subsequent reader challenge. Nearly five hundred readers participated, and many stated that the reason they had the courage to participate was because their self-portrait could be whimsical and unrealistic.

The artwork in this book takes creative self-portraits a step further, showing that you can make a self-portrait—with or without your physical likeness—in any form, from books and dolls to journals and collages. Even more exciting, you'll discover your own creative process while exploring the various viewpoints and projects of the artists featured in the following pages.

As children, often our very first drawings are of ourselves. That unabashed and innocent self-centeredness permitted in very young children flourishes within us still. We hope this book will help you find it and bring it out for all to see.

CATE COULACOS PRATO

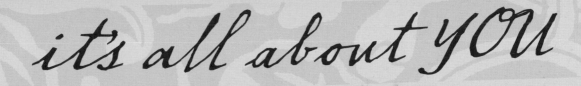

it's all about YOU

The importance of the artist's self-portrait

SELF-PORTRAITS. Where else can an artist be absolutely indulgent and self-absorbed? A self-portrait is your one-way ticket to the land of **YOU**! It's a place where you can see your beauty, understand your shadows, and express deep, intense, and painful emotions. It's a powerful tool, one that can effect change and growth, tell stories, and promote connections with others with an invitation to view your unconditional self. As an artist, your career in self-portraits will allow endless experimentation with the physical elements of art, but also will lead you to a gateway of alternate realities, to the person you fantasize about being or want to become.

In the pages that follow, you can get a glimpse at famous self-portraiture artists, such as van Gogh, and find inspirational quotes. Take a peek inside the personal journeys of the artists who wrote about the therapeutic benefits of creating a self-portrait. Finally, read the compelling essays of several artists brave enough to show and tell. All in all, self-portraiture is going to make you a better artist. This chapter will begin to show you how.

> **"Of course I'm enjoying myself, there's no one else here to enjoy."**
>
> **— OSCAR WILDE,**
>   **in response to an inquiry from**
>   **his hostess at a party.**

THE HISTORY OF *self-portraits*

Leon Battista Alberti (who was, quite literally, one of the original Renaissance men) credited the beginning of self-portraits—in fact, of all portraiture—to the moment when Narcissus saw his reflection in a pool of water and "trembled at the beauty of his own face." Though Narcissus is the stuff of myths, it is likely that self-portraits have been around for as long as humans have recognized their reflection. There is evidence that the ancient Greeks and Egyptians carved self-portraits in stone as art and signatures on their work. But the genre really took off with the advent of mirrors in the fifteenth century.

Many of the world's most famous artworks are self-portraits. Rembrandt used self-portraits to chronicle his life. Van Dyck used them to enhance his image—socially and physically. Van Gogh used them to express his emotions. Chagall and Picasso told stories through theirs. Frida Kahlo used them to work out her issues—physical, emotional, and political.

In the twentieth century, photography became important in self-portraiture, with Andy Warhol posing moodily for the large-format Polaroid camera and Cindy Sherman disappearing into the roles of B-movie heroines through makeup and costuming.

famous self-portrait artists

Study the work of these artists to uncover various viewpoints of this important art form.

FRIDA KAHLO (MEXICAN, 1907–1954) Kahlo created fifty-five self-portraits, many of which helped her express physical and emotional issues.

VINCENT VAN GOGH (DUTCH, 1853–1890) Vincent van Gogh painted twenty-two self-portraits, most of them completed during the last years of his life. As his life and his art progressed, his frustrations with both—as well as his severe form of epilepsy and mental illness—are reflected in his work.

REMBRANDT VAN RIJN (DUTCH, 1606–1669) Rembrandt was a prolific artist, creating some ninety self-portraits, from youth to old age. From his body of work, art critics and historians conclude that he made self-portraits for several reasons: because he was a ready model; in order to experiment—sketching himself with different facial expressions (some quite comical), hairstyles, and clothes; and as a way to record his life.

ANTHONY VAN DYCK (FLEMISH, 1599–1641) According to art critics and historians, van Dyck liked to use his self-portraits not only as a way to show off his artistic talent, but to promote himself socially. In his Self-Portrait, thought to be painted around 1620, young van Dyck is sending a message to viewers—and possible patrons. He makes no reference to himself as an artist just gaining popularity. Instead, his posture, gestures, and clothing, as well as the setting make him look like a prosperous gentleman, self-conscious of his position.

Self-Portrait, completed in 1887, is typical of van Gogh's work near the end of his life. The colors of the hat and jacket are vivid. The brushstrokes are staccato and frenzied, creating whorls of movement in different directions. Compared to his earlier dark and sedate self-portraits, this one is all feeling and expression: it shows the artist like a meteor flashing bright against the sky, with one last burst of light before it burns out. *Image courtesy of The Detroit Institute of Arts.*

SELF-PORTRAITURE *today*

In the twenty-first century, websites and blogs are the studios and galleries of our time. Artists' websites and blogs offer the same wonderful duality of a self-portrait by juxtaposing the notion of intimacy with bold publicity. These digital forums are, at their core, about self-discovery and self-promotion. So it is no surprise that a weekly online self-portrait project that started in 2006 has become so wildly popular in the cyber-art community. When viewing the project, you will find artists talking about how shy they are or how silly they feel taking self-portrait pictures with food or bathroom themes. Yet they do it en masse, fulfilling one of the goals that project pioneer and photo-media artist Kathreen Ricketson had at the outset of the project. She wanted to encourage people to push their personal boundaries and cast off inhibitions while also giving self-expression a forum and a community.

Whether the self-portraits of the Renaissance or on today's blogs are an act of exhibitionism or an act of courage is absolutely up for discussion. But the reasons why we make self-portraits are timeless. Just look at the artists in this book, and you'll see why.

blog to become a better artist

Web journals are a great way to improve your skills and gain exposure.

A weblog—an online journal commonly known as a blog—can increase your self-awareness, promote yourself and your art, and serve as a record of your progress as an artist. Many artists have found that blogging connects them with a community of artists (a supportive lifeline when you're toiling away in your lonely studio). It also helps them get noticed by galleries, publishers, and art collectors (Money! Fame!). Plus, who doesn't want to play show-and-tell with their art?

It's easy to start a blog, even if you're a technophobe, and relatively inexpensive. Some services, such as Blogger, Google's hosting website, are free. Others charge according to the kinds of features to which you subscribe. But whether you sign on with a basic blog or one with all the bells and whistles, there are some basic rules for success.

Check out your options In addition to learning about prices and feature options from blog-hosting services, look at other artists' blogs and determine what you like and don't like about the overall look of the blog and the ease of its use. Many artists prefer blog sites that allow them more latitude for creativity with layouts and photographs while making it easy for visitors to comment. Bloggers love to talk about their blogs, so feel free to contact them to ask what they like and don't like about their service.

Dive in The best way to start a blog is to just do it. Most art blogs evolve over time, and attention spans on the Internet are short. One thing you should give some thought to, however, is the blog's name. If you don't know exactly what it's "about" yet, just think of something clever, succinct, and memorable that says "you."

Post pictures Artists are visual; pictures attract them. Pictures of your art, your adorable kids, your flower garden, the seashells from your vacation—it's all eye candy for the visitor. Good pictures will excite and inspire readers and keep them coming back for more. Great pictures will have them commenting and telling other people about your blog.

Post often If people like your blog, they'll come back. If they keep coming back to the same old, stale post day after day—or week after week—they'll move on. You'll want to post at least once a week, and preferably two to three times a week or more.

Advertise Don't hide your blog under a bushel: let people know about it by e-mailing your friends and relatives—even your friends' relatives—and inviting them to visit your new blog. Another good way to get people to visit your blog is to comment on other people's blogs with a link to yours. Curious readers will click on the link to get to your blog. You should also add links to other blogs you like with the hope that those bloggers will return the favor.

"I Don't Wear Hats, but I'm Fine with My Tiara" by Karen Fricke, 2005

Karen made this mixed-media self-portrait in response to a reader challenge in *Quilting Arts Magazine*. "The fuchsia hair shows no signs of gray, and my love of color is reflected in my complexion. My earrings dangle my passions—sewing and gardening, but the true jewels of my life are my 'cute as buttons' children: Michael, Megan, Sarah, and Katie."

8½" w × 11" h (21.5 × 28 cm)

the benefits of creating SELF-PORTRAITS

Over time, artists have turned to self-portraiture to study their craft and to explore and express themselves. A self-portrait is without boundaries, allowing artists to portray themselves as they wish to be seen. They are also invitations to connect with the artist on a deeper level, allowing others to peer inside and see aspects both hidden and in full view. On a practical note, self-portraits give the artist a ready-made, always available (not to mention cheap) model on whom to experiment with light, color, shadow, and the human form and often serve as advertisement for the kind of work they do.

"I Want You for U.S. Army" by James Montgomery Flagg is arguably one of the most popular poster images in history. The poster was originally created to help the war effort after the United States entered World War I. When the image was later adapted for World War II, Flagg admitted to using his own likeness as the model for Uncle Sam to save money.

THEY SAID IT *themselves*

If you are looking for reasons, comfort, or perhaps mantras to inspire your foray into self-portraiture, you may find a place of solace in the quotes listed here. Heed the words from the experts: journeying into the self will not present an easy path, but the fruit of the rewards can be the greatest ever achieved.

"Every portrait that is painted with feeling is a portrait of the artist, not of the sitter. The sitter is merely an accident, the occasion. It is not he who is revealed by the painter; it is rather the painter who, on the colored canvas, reveals himself."
—Oscar Wilde

**"THE SELF IS A PROJECT, SOMETHING TO BE BUILT."
—SUSAN SONTAG**

"I loathe my own face, and I've done self-portraits because I've had nobody else to do."

—Francis Bacon

"Since my subjects have always been my sensations, my states of mind and the profound reactions that life has been producing in me, I have frequently objectified all this in figures of myself, which were the most sincere and real thing that I could do in order to express what I felt inside and outside of myself."

—Frida Kahlo

**"[THE ARTIST] IS A MODEL WHO IS ALWAYS READY, OFFERING ALL THE ADVANTAGES; HE COMES ON TIME, HE DOES WHAT YOU TELL HIM, AND YOU ALREADY KNOW HIM BEFORE YOU START TO PAINT HIM."
—Henri Fantin-Latour**

"Every artist dips his brush in his own soul, and paints his own nature into his pictures."
—Henry Ward Beecher

"It is important to express oneself...provided the feelings are real and taken from your own experience."
—Berthe Morisot

"I should not talk so much about myself if there were anybody else whom I knew as well."
—Henry David Thoreau

"Painting is just another way of keeping a diary."
—Pablo Picasso

"Normal is in the eye of the beholder."
—Whoopi Goldberg

"I paint self-portraits because I am so often alone, because I am the person I know best."
—Frida Kahlo

"All artists are vain, they long to be recognized and to leave something to posterity. They want to be loved, and at the same time they want to be free. But nobody is free."
—Francis Bacon

"The reason that I'm an actor, or an artist, is ultimately because I'm trying to paint a self-portrait, and the most complete and beautiful self-portrait that [I] can."
—Terrence Howard

"I loathe narcissism, but I approve of vanity."
—Diana Vreeland

Artist Kathie Briggs created this quilted piece for the *Quilting Arts Magazine* creative self-portrait challenge in 2005. This mixed-media quilt was her response to having just received a rejection letter. She wanted to hole up and lick her wounds, but was scheduled to teach a workshop. She pasted on a smile, but inside felt sad—the self-portrait is a snapshot of how she felt that day.

8½" w × 11" h (21.5 × 28 cm)

ART *therapy*

Whether you're angry, grief-stricken, mortified, or overcome by feelings you just can't put a name to, art therapy can help. Somehow, like writing in a journal, making art allows the feelings to come out safely—no matter how wild, painful, or murderous. Once the feelings have been expressed and are contained on the page—or the canvas—you feel calmer. With art, you have the option of being able to express your feelings in color with long, flowing lines that calm or staccato stabs that vent. You can crush clay into submission or release your feelings while you rip paper. A therapeutic self-portrait allows you to express exactly how you feel. On the pages that follow, you can see one artist's variations on her own self-portrait, which shows her innocent youth.

therapeutic SELF-PORTRAITS

By Linda Edkins Wyatt

You can treat a portrait on paper or fabric in a way that would be dangerous for a human—gouge out an eye, cut a hole in the heart, splatter the face with bleach, dribble blood-red paint, ooze green, bilious goop out of an ear or mouth. You can elongate and twist the neck or wrap it with wire or twine to indicate a feeling of choking. You might even let an eyeball hang from its socket. Cutting up a photo and reassembling it in an unnatural way can illustrate feelings of confusion—an eye on the nose area, an ear where a mouth should be. You can add strong words coming out of the mouth, illustrate steam coming out of the ears with Angelina fibers or cotton puffs, split the head open and show the vulnerability of your gray matter. You can even zipper the mouth shut or hammer in brads or studs around a feature. A tiny head and a large, distorted body can illustrate feelings of people not taking your words and ideas seriously; in contrast, a huge head carried by a tiny, weakened body can illustrate feelings of carrying a heavy emotional burden and having too much on your mind. An unnaturally large or small body can show that you wrestle with body-image issues.

These "disturbed" portraits can help you in several ways. First, they get your feelings out. Simply expressing the troubling emotions that you feel can jump-start the healing process. Ignoring the negative feelings or glossing over them just makes the pain and hurt go deeper within you and fester. Art lets negative feelings out in a healthy way.

You aren't obligated to show the portraits to anyone. However, sharing them with people who care about you, such as close family members, good friends, therapists, or spiritual leaders can start a healing dialogue. Other family members, especially children, might be encouraged to do their own therapeutic self-portraits or even their portrayal of you.

One of the easiest and most satisfying ways to create your altered self-portrait is to manipulate a photo with image-editing software, such as Adobe Photoshop. I began with an idea of taking one photo and giving it many different treatments to express a variety of emotions, moods, and eras. I settled on using my college gradua-tion photo, taken way back in 1977. I scanned the photo and then began to play with the image. While digitally editing, I discovered that if I explored the Filter menu and its submenus, there were several exciting options. I tried out quite a few, and the results were both surprising and inspiring.

7½"w x 10"h (19 x 25 cm)

7½" w × 10" h (19 × 25 cm)

SCARY

I dramatized shadows and bags under my eyes with shades of purple and pink in this piece and added lines around my mouth to convey the feelings of unhappiness, emotional or physical abuse, sadness, loneliness, ill health, loss, and depression that many people experience. To achieve a similar look, use the following menu path: Filter>Artistic>Cutout. Lightly heated Tyvek, painted with drab shades of green, copper, and silver, was stitched to the right side. It amplifies the feeling of distress and is reminiscent of war-zone camouflage. The zigzag stitching over the mouth and on the neck suggests a person not being able to speak up or being afraid of the resulting consequences. Watercolors, markers, and colored pencils were also used.

INNOCENCE

I wanted this piece to appear as if it had been done with a woodcut or linoleum block. Under the Filter menu, I chose Sketch>Stamp. The resulting image looked like an old photo with a grayish, sketched appearance. I printed the image out onto textured watercolor paper, sprayed it with fixative, and then added soft pinks and peaches in the background with watercolor to convey gentleness and innocence. I added cut pieces of fused Angelina fibers in lavender shades at the neck and in the upper right corner for additional femininity. Pieces cut from recycled textured facial cleansing cloth, painted with gold acrylic, were adhered to illustrate my once-lustrous hair. I left the face untouched to infer innocence and inexperience. All areas except the face were randomly quilted with pink thread. This piece shows my budding interest in the world of textiles with the use of textured gold fiber and Angelina, yet the untreated face infers that I had not yet experienced much on my life's path.

7½"w × 10"h (19 × 25 cm)

digital imaging tips

Use the following tips to create no-fail mixed-media self-portraits with digital images.

✦ Whether altering images digitally or by hand, always work on duplicate photos. That way, if you make a mistake, you still have the original. Some image-editing programs, such as the Photoshop family, have a History palette that lists every edit you make to a digital file. This allows you to retrace your steps so that you don't have to start over if you are unhappy with your results.

✦ If you like the effect of a filter on the photo, save the resulting image with a new name that includes the filter so you can remember how you did it. You can also organize your favorite filters inside most image-editing programs.

✦ It's a good idea to spray photos with fixative before applying paint. Ink-jet printer inks tend to bleed when they are exposed to water or watercolor paints.

✦ Paper can be sewn, but you should stabilize it before running it through the sewing machine. Back papers with strong fabric to strengthen them before any sewing is attempted. Use a longer stitch length than usual so the paper won't fall apart.

✦ Images can also be printed on fabrics. You can buy print-ready fabrics at your local fabric or craft store; they feed through the printer just like paper. You can also print on fabrics of your choice if you stabilize the fabric first. You can iron freezer paper to the wrong side of the fabric to give it stability and peel it off when you are finished. Avoid using synthetic fabrics in your printer. Also, be sure to trim rough edges and loose threads that can get caught in the printer mechanisms.

7½"w × 10"h (19 × 25 cm)

MIME

The idea here was to express the way women use makeup to either enhance their beauty or cover up imperfections. I used the college photo, printed on textured watercolor paper, without any filter. Half the face was painted with white acrylic and has elaborate rainbow eye makeup applied with watercolors, acrylics, colored pencils, and markers. The left side has a less dramatic eye treatment; the skin seems red and irritated, with tired and pale eyes, and stitches to indicate wrinkles and fatigue. It begs the question "What is hiding behind the painted face?"

7½"w × 10"h (19 × 25 cm)

THIRD EYE

For many people, a way to get out of an unhappy frame of mind is to explore feelings both deep inside themselves and in the universe, through religion or other spiritual journeys. This piece has a clean, bright, fun look with crisp colors, geometric shapes, and confetti-inspired designs. However, the insertion of a third eye on the forehead suggests looking deeply within oneself and examining your own spirituality and creative nature in order to overcome negativity and fulfill your creative potential. The lack of hair gives it a New Age look inspired by artist Alex Grey. Acrylic paints, markers, and colored pencils were used. No filters were applied to the photo.

7½" w × 10"h (19 × 25 cm)

TWISTED

I wanted to express how life can overwhelm people and pull them in many directions, leaving them rattled, confused, and off-kilter. Under the Filter menu, I chose Distort>Twist. Suddenly my face was skewed and deformed. Again I printed the image out on textured watercolor paper and sprayed it with fixative. Next I added jarring, fiery, red-orange hair to show alarm, and used a contrasting shade of lime green to accent it. After stabilizing the piece with heavy cotton, I used bright orange topstitching thread to accent the eyes and hair and lime green zigzag stitching on the neck and hairline.

art therapy resources

Art is a wonderful means for anyone to express themselves, but for those who have suffered emotional disturbances, trauma, or physical pain, art can be a way to heal. Look to these resources for more information.

AMERICAN ART THERAPY ASSOCIATION
(arttherapy.org) Clearinghouse of information and resources for both art therapists and those interested in learning more about art therapy.

ARTS AND HEALING NETWORK (artheals.org)
Online resource for anyone interested in the healing power of art.

NATIONAL COALITION OF CREATIVE ARTS THERAPIES ASSOCIATIONS (nccata.org) Alliance of professional associations dedicated to the advancement of art as therapy.

SOCIETY FOR THE ARTS IN HEALTHCARE
(thesah.org) Nonprofit organization dedicated to promoting the inclusion of art as an integral component in healthcare.

SELF-HELP HEALING ARTS JOURNAL
(self-help-healing-arts-journal.com) Artist website furthering belief that art journaling can help heal the soul and emotional wounds, reclaim your inner artist, and improve self-esteem.

ART THERAPY (art-therapy.us) Site organized by a leading art therapist full of information for experts and those wishing to know more about art therapy.

ART THERAPY CONNECTION
(arttherapyconnection.org) Not-for-profit organization dedicated to helping at-risk children succeed in school.

7½" w × 10" h (19 × 25 cm)

LOST

This piece shows a shadowy face floating without a body or hair. I chose pinkish newsprint from a financial publication to indicate the media's overwhelming and often frightening influence and some recycled vegetable net to express a feeling of being trapped or closed out from society. The shimmering Angelina fibers wrap around the head, hinting at the person's mental-health problems hiding under the cocoonlike wrap. Under the Filter menu, I chose Artistic>Neon Glow. The altered photo was printed on textured watercolor paper, lightly enhanced with colored pencil, and stitched.

7½" w × 10" h (19 × 25 cm)

WARHOL

This piece is loosely based on Andy Warhol's Pop Art silk-screened portraits of famous celebrities. Some people are blessed with self-confidence. Others struggle with their own identity and self-esteem. To celebrate a newly strengthened sense of self, I painted on a printed image. Before printing, I altered the image by using Filter>Artistic>Cutout to achieve a graphic look. By using acrylic fabric paint in bold shades of purple, turquoise, and gold, I overpainted the photo, and enhanced the planes, lines, and shadows of my face. Thus I accented and strengthened the image of me, enhancing basic features such as my cheekbones, eye socket, hairline, and chin. This portrait says, "I am me. I am bold, and I accept myself for who I am."

7½" w × 10"h (19 × 25 cm)

PSYCHEDELIC

On this piece I used the following menu path: Filter>Stylize>Trace Contour. The stiff, posed college photo suddenly became lines and dots of colorful turquoise, magenta, and green, and inspired me to try a dreamlike, Pop Art, late-1960s look. I printed the photo on textured watercolor paper, sprayed it with fixative, and then added turquoise in the background and bright orange on the right side of the face with watercolor paints. I added some touches of yellow on the eyes, hair, and neck. Next I glued a thin strip of a gold-painted disposable face cloth down the center, randomly adding gold squares and rectangles. I stabilized the work with heavy cotton fabric before I began stitching with pink thread. I did a random stitch on the background and heavily accented the eyes and eyelashes with pink thread to add to the young, girlish feeling and to suggest a psychedelic way of seeing the world. The bright, clean colors are reminiscent of the late-1960s Summer of Love. The dotted texture makes it feel dreamy, and the gold pieces add to the magical feeling.

Self-portrait projects can lead to definite closure. In the above example, artist Juliana Coles used art to deal with an incredibly painful past. Through her journal, she vows not to be a product of this tragedy, but instead to live the life she wishes to lead and be the soul she wishes to be.

1"h × 16"w (31 × 41 cm)
Extreme visual journaling with collage and mixed media

"This brutal self-portrait is the tale of my mother as myself, and her legacy is what I try to unlearn and un-live in order to be who I truly am. It's her story, not mine. Truth is the key that I will find in my journals, page after page, book after book."

—Juliana

i grew up in BLUEBEARD'S CASTLE

By Juliana Coles

The purpose of keeping an extreme visual journal as a self-portrait is to know thyself. I incorporate text with imagery to create an internal dialogue between my higher power or ancient self, who contacts me through signs and symbols, and my contemporary self, who connects through language. I use mixed media in unknown ways as a bridge to the unconscious. The raw expression from my interior is more important to me than making a pretty picture that others will accept and call art.

The Motherline as a theme is a very significant golden thread leading me to who I am.

In this disturbing two-page spread, I cut up some old black-and-white copies of photographs of my mother as a young woman and then put them back together, just to see how they might appear in this new perspective. The human face, when carefully studied as in a self-portrait, is really not symmetrical at all. These two sides of one are so compellingly different and these differences interest me like a life map or some sort of facial geometry. Below my mother, I added some more black-and-white graphic images of two men whom I don't know. I was trying to create new relationships between the images to see where it would take me.

I don't direct or manipulate my work but rather attempt to let it reveal its own nature. What I do is mess around, trying different ideas and techniques until I like the result or decide to start over. In this piece, I cut the whole thing up into strips and then randomly glued them down—but it didn't fit in the book, so I had to put it in sideways. I added more paint and then some journaling to try and find out more about the piece and what it wanted to tell me. I scanned it and printed a copy from the computer and glued it on the other page, frontally. Somehow with the strips it appeared like a flag to me.

Like many of my favorite artists, such as Jasper Johns and Rauschenberg, in my early artistic life I often used the stars and stripes to break up space. So, in the top half I added my old-school stars and again played with paint, colored markers, and rubber stamps for patterns. Then, creating more stripes with white ink, I did some writing across the body of the figures when it hit me and I added the title *I Grew Up in Bluebeard's Castle*. Clarissa Pinkola Estes has a great rendition of the classic Bluebeard fairy tale in her book *Women Who Run With the Wolves*. The uninitiated bride marries a horrible murdering monster and in doing so, must never ask who he is, what this little key is for, or, for that matter, who she is. I thought of my fearful mother and my dangerous father, and I knew oh I knew, I had grown up in Bluebeard's castle. In discovering the key, I added my old address, that dreadful house, in rubber-stamped letters, redrawing them to make them look like my own hand. I added more texture and more writing.

This brutal self-portrait is the tale of my mother as myself, and her legacy is what I try to unlearn and unlive in order to be who I truly am. It's her story, not mine. Truth is the key that I will find in my journals, page after page, book after book. It's my gift to myself and my unfolding. It's hauntingly beautiful, tragic, joyous, and my greatest triumph. Reveal your Self to the light of your pages. Otherwise, the dead bodies in the basement pile up. Me, I go to meet them and ask them who they are or tell them to get the hell out of my house. The light is in the darkness. I choose to see me in all my pain and glory. Eventually, we all have to ask ourselves what the key is for in order to begin our own path of initiation: an endless experiment in self-portraiture and personal mythology.

feel the PAIN

The first stab at self-portraiture can cut incredibly deeply. It takes no small amount of courage to seek inside the soul and pull out all the ugly. But, often, it is through the pain and shadow that we see the light and the beauty. What follows are four artists' first experiments with self-portraiture. All tackle the agony of acutely looking at their so-called physical flaws. The first artist used self-deprecating humor to lighten her load while the second takes you into her past and allows you to experience the pain of growing up overweight. The third and fourth are from a pair of sisters, one focusing on her middle age, the other taking stock of her life.

reflections of a SELF-PORTRAIT
By Cheryl Prater

I have to admit, I had never considered creating a self-portrait. First of all, I'm not a real artist, and painting oneself is an exercise for real artists. You know who real artists are, don't you? Real artists use oil paints and cut off their ears and wear red turbans. Real artists create self-portraits because they are their own most compliant and available models. They use their own image to do studies in light, chronicle themselves over time, or record themselves at work. Real artists are extremely talented, somewhat tortured, and mostly dead. I am only one of these things.

The only reason I confront my reflection is to put on my makeup or to make sure I don't have a piece of oregano lodged in my front teeth. What the heck do I need with a self-portrait? Driver's license photographs and age have cured me of any vanity I once had. Other people can look at me, but I don't want to look at me, okay?

Yet here I sit, facing my reflection in an effort to give it a try. Should I smile? Look serious? Wrap a bandage around my head? What about a profile? Maybe I'll look like a Ralph Lauren model if I pose like this.

NOPE.

Why? Because I have something that Ralph Lauren models don't have: a bunch of floppy business under my chin. Bet they're jealous.

This is a painful process. Creating a portrait of myself is like making a topographical map showing the routes to all my flaws and imperfections, complete with detours to self-conscious points-of-interest. Unwanted Facial Hair Forest and Chickenpox Scar Gorge, next exit. Be sure to pick up a souvenir at the Age Spot Gift Shop! Huge buffet with free sundaes for the kiddies at the Crow's Feet Cafe!

Facing the mirror, I am confronted with the reality that I am starting to show signs of the miles I've logged. That crease I used to get when I'd furrow my brow? It's now a permanent forehead feature regardless of my expression. Laugh lines? Not funny. What if I pull my face upward? Maybe I can make it look like it did twenty years of gravity ago? Uh, no. This doesn't make me look younger; it makes me look like I'm in perpetual reaction to being ambushed. In a wind tunnel.

This would be so much easier if I could make this self-portrait of someone else. Someone whose left eyebrow isn't about 20 percent larger than the right one. Someone more symmetrical, with smaller pores. Someone who doesn't have these tiny white spots all over—oh, wait, that's toothpaste spatter on the mirror. Never mind.

So. One last glance in the mirror before giving up on this exercise and grabbing the facial wax and Windex. Just need to check—hey! Why didn't you tell me I had oregano in my front teeth?

"*Facing the mirror, I am confronted with the reality that I am starting to show signs of the miles I've logged.*"
—Cheryl

Cheryl found digital images of famous self-portraits and digitally altered them by replacing the artists' faces with her own.

15"w × 9½"h × 1"d (38 × 24 × 3 cm)
Digital collage and assemblage

20" w × 30" h (51 × 76 cm) Mixed-media collage with paint and paper

"The real challenge for the self-portrait artist is not whether to reveal the wrinkles, the fat, and the whiskers, but whom to reveal."

—Loretta

This piece shows the artist as a young girl at her first communion, crowned with gilded book pages. She is wearing her "many-layered" dress (here made out of folded tissue paper and paper lace) decorated with titles from some of her favorite books since childhood, reflecting stages of her life, from *The Borrowers* and *Black Beauty* to *The Edible Woman* and *Writing Down the Bones*.

MY BODY, not myself

By Loretta Benedetto Marvel

The prospect of creating a self-portrait in middle age is daunting. I never have used my body as the subject of my work. In fact, the first essay I wrote to accompany this artwork ignored the issue, dwelling on my "interior life," reading about life instead of living it.

I'd prefer to airily dismiss the whole physical thing by saying that middle age has brought me peace with the issues of wrinkles, pounds, and gray hair, but I cannot. The one thing I have learned through the years is that you can't make art with a lie. The false note is always the one that is heard the loudest.

My mind and body live separate lives. Why meld the two now? From an early age, my body caused me nothing but shame, most of which I can attribute to being raised as a good Italian-American Catholic girl. Although the "sins of the flesh" were very real to me as a child, I didn't really have the slightest idea of what they were! I can't lay the entire blame for my self-flagellation on the red slippers of the Pope, though. If I had been a thin, pretty girl instead of a fat, dumpy girl, I may have felt less repressed. Yes, I was a total cliché: overweight, bookish, and a nerd.

I learned to stay on the fringes and became an observer of the world both through books and over the tops of them. It was easy to peer at my classmates when they thought I was reading and my social awkwardness was diffused by preoccupation. My creative life blossomed when I discovered my observances could be fodder for stories.

So I developed my artistic voice not despite my dysfunctional body image but because of it. For as much as I reveal to you in my art, the layers are there to hide what I keep in the dark. I see the real world through stories told over cups of tea and smoky fires. My art is a fairy tale that hinges on the use of icons and make-believe relationships both past and future. My art is stitched through with layers of narrative thread that is at times as obvious as French knots and at other times as understated as a blind hem. Sometimes the layers can bury the true image deeply, disguising it with paint and collage and gold leaf and buttons and the remnants of life that others clean out from dusty vanity drawers and throw into the waste can. This is where my "shadow self" resides, the one that I try to keep tightly under wraps. This is the self who wonders how she arrived at this place in her life, where she commands courtrooms by day and has the respect of judges and adversaries, but still keeps that book in her bag in case she has to eat lunch by herself.

The authentic challenge in creating a self-portrait in middle age is that all of the above is true and yet none of it is and that all these selves are equally authentic and yet totally false, depending on the day, the mood, or the moon. The real challenge for the self-portrait artist is not whether to reveal the wrinkles, the fat, and the whiskers, but whom to reveal.

And so it comes down to this: In the authentic portrait of the self that is fixed in my mind's eye, I am always in the sunshine on the grass, clothed in a many-layered dress sewn by my mother's hand, neither fat nor thin, and forever young. In the self-portrait I create for the world to see and judge, I hide my sins and appetite behind my intellect, splaying all the books I've ever read across me like my grandma's apron, hoping it will give me the same legitimacy. In the self-portrait of my lifetime, I stand iconic, with the sea billowing around my shoulders, caressing me like a veil of tears mixed with ocean spray, with my love of the written word crowning my head, and in my hands, a book, of course, so that I may maintain a facade of indifference while on view, pretending to read the words, but all the while sneaking a look beyond it into the face of the unknown.

AGING *gracefully*

By Allison Stilwell

I always thought that I would age gracefully, embracing the changes and bumps we inevitably hit as we get older—like needing glasses, unwanted wrinkles, and achy joints. However, I hate it. I can hardly believe I am that older person in the mirror. I hate to admit it, but it has been a real struggle to age gracefully. This was what I was thinking about as I worked on my self-portrait.

I dug through my old drawings to find a self-portrait I sketched for a college class about fifteen years ago. I scanned it into my computer, resized it, printed it out, and colored it with colored pencils. I purposely tried to use unnaturally bright colors. When I was happy with the results, I used this drawing as a map for my fabric face.

As I "painted with fabric," I sat with a pile of scraps and cut pieces of fabric to re-create my image. I built the face by pinning the fabric directly to a light cotton bat. Once satisfied, I took the image to the sewing machine and free sewed it with variegated thread. I then said a small prayer and threw it in with my laundry.

When my self-portrait came out of the dryer, she was old, raggedy, wrinkly, and perfectly aged, but her eyes were a bit wild and her mouth had a strange tilt. Oh no, she needed plastic surgery. So I took her back to the studio and went over her fabric face with Cray-Pas or oil sticks to raise her eyes, re-form her mouth a bit, and add punches of color that were lost in the wash. I then took her back to the sewing machine to add detail with black stitching. I also added some more color by adding some stitching with bright rayon thread.

The box was painted with acrylic paint. I painted the inside with different colors of crackle paint. I also distressed the paint by sanding and scraping it. I added words with rubber stamps and distressing inks. I used a woodcarving tool to dig lines through the paint around her head. I added checkerboards with acrylic paint.

The juxtaposition of the original drawing that artist
Allison Stilwell created while in college with the distressed
fabric rendering makes a visual statement about how the artist
sees herself in her present state. The vivid color, although still
there, is cracked and withered by the years.

12"w × 12"h × 2"d (31 × 31 × 5 cm)
Mixed-media collage with fabric, wood frame, and paint

Trying to Age Gracefully

SELF-PORTRAIT 2007

By Tracy Stilwell

The self-portrait project allowed me to present the loves of my life (most of them) and the reminders of peace and personal bravery using bits of those special mixed materials I keep carrying around: a small transferred photo of myself as a child, two very small plastic babies symbolizing my children who have grown into men, a mention of my "what would I do without her" girlfriend Sue, the garden, where we spend endless hours digging, moving dirt, plants, trees, rocks for fun and pleasure. Then there is the underlying and always challenging work of just being: being calm, accepting, and grateful; being centered and open; being responsible for myself; being grateful again and again.

This project started by scanning a charcoal drawing of myself (from my first and only drawing class) into the computer to create a digital image. After resizing the piece, it was printed onto photo transfer paper and ironed onto muslin. I used chalks, pencils, and watercolor pencils to add color to the face and background of the photo transfer. The black-and-white background cloth was pieced together from black fabric that had been discharged with bleach.

After machine stitching the face onto the discharged material, I went through fabric scraps and picked out words and images that spoke to me and machine stitched them in place.

I pulled beads, flowers, the little plastic babies, buttons, rubber-stamped shrink plastic pieces, and other goodies from my collection of "things." These items were all hand stitched on. I used images and trinkets that reflected things that I love and hold dear. The embellished face was affixed to a piece of foam core and attached to the inside of the box.

The wooden box was from the "stuff" collection picked up at a flea market. Prior to inserting the cloth face, I painted the outside of the box just to darken, not to actually cover, the wood. Then I painted big dots on top of the black with watered-down white paint. Having been gifted with a container of shell rounds from a defunct button factory, I glued some to the edge of the box.

The graphics for the inside edges of the box started with a plain piece of watercolor paper. I gathered scrap papers, cut-out words, images, a sign from a driver in England that had "THE GIRLZ" written in big black letters, gel medium, an old credit card for spreading the medium, and brown and black distressing inks. I drew the needed shapes on the paper and proceeded to collage with the papers and medium. The distressing inks toned down the papers and helped blend the mixed papers. The inks can be applied directly and wiped around, or with a foam applicator. The pieces were cut to size and glued into place.

The thing that I loved the most about this particular project is that I had a chance to use my head, heart, and hands to create something with the materials I had within reach.

Self-portraits do not always have to count the flaws or the wrinkles. They can be abstract representations of your life, your challenges, your accomplishments. This piece by Tracy Stilwell expresses her loves.

12"w × 16"h × 2½"d
Mixed-media collage with found objects, wood frame, and paint

DECIMAL EQUIVALENTS OF MI...

propel
propel
provide
promise
proper

Good morning, Goody Two-Shoes."

The Rational Idea

know thyself

IT WOULD BE NICE if you could just sit down and make the perfect self-portrait. But if you could, you probably wouldn't be reading this book. It's okay, you're bound to be a little nervous, a little self-conscious, a little "where do I start?" This chapter is designed to help you explore, loosen up, learn a few tricks of the trade. It will also show you that every artist has her or his own approach. And most struggle with the same hang-ups of discovering themselves and then capturing what they want to express in art.

The warm-ups are designed to help you get to know yourself in a variety of ways so you have raw material from which to draw—do as many or as few as you like. Next come some practical approaches to working with the face—drawing faces and eyes, the essence of a physical self-portrait—and a digital option. After you've gleaned some practical information, you can think about the creative process of designing a self-portrait by reading three different spins from three different artists.

> **"The mirror, above all—
> the mirror is our teacher."**
> **— LEONARDO DA VINCI**

37

These are exercises to stretch your creative muscle and ease any tension or anxiety you feel about yourself and the process of creating a self-portrait. The goal is to reveal information about yourself. And you can turn off the perfectionist—these are just exercises. Think of them as doodles. However, you may want to keep track of your findings in a journal or even do the exercises directly in your journal for future reference.

color YOUR WORLD

Are you blue? Do you see red? Green with envy? Choose a color and make a self-portrait using only that shade. It can be a literal self-portrait of your face and/or body or an abstract or expressive self-portrait. To make the experience more interesting, visually and intellectually, consider using different media in the hue of your choice.

+ Fabrics (consider patterns, luminosity, nap, and grain as you choose them)

+ Paints, pastels, or markers

+ Found papers, scrapbook papers, painted-over newsprint, wallpaper, cut-up magazine pages

+ Photographs manipulated and "colored" with digital darkroom techniques

+ Plant materials

+ Felt and other fibers

+ Found objects

The results of this exercise depend on your current state of mind and will therefore vary depending on your mood. For best results, do this exercise in one sitting, as your mood, and therefore your "color," may change if you stop and come back another time. More important, pay attention to how you work. For example, as you work in one color, you may discover that the hue doesn't suit you at all, and you gravitate toward a different color. This tells you something about yourself. Feel free to explore another color or stick with the first color to bring up feelings of why it doesn't "work" for you. Record your findings.

"I found I could say things with color and shapes that I couldn't say any other way— things I had no words for."
—Georgia O'Keeffe

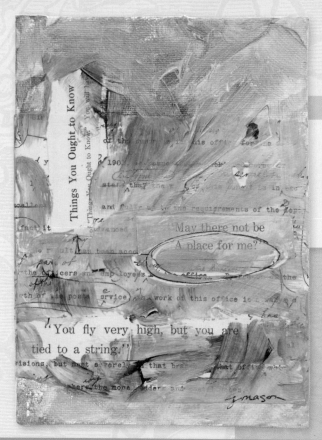

The three pieces of artwork on this and the following two pages by Jenn Mason show how you can use color to explore various moods. This piece, *Feeling Tied to a String*, demonstrates anxiety through orange.

5"w × 7"h (13 × 18 cm), mixed-media collage on canvas

color symbolism

Colors symbolize feelings, stature, and celebration in most every culture—though the meaning can change from one culture to the next and even change within a culture over time. Here are some other symbolic associations with colors:

BLUE

POSITIVE: Steady, secure (blue-chip stocks); peaceful, calming (a clear sky and the lulling ocean)

NEGATIVE: Sadness (singing the blues); evil (blue devils)

RED

POSITIVE: Success and celebration (red-letter day, roll out the red carpet)

NEGATIVE: Anger (seeing red); injury (blood); embarrassment (red-faced)

YELLOW

POSITIVE: Happiness, sunshine (a sunny outlook)

NEGATIVE: Cowardice (yellow-bellied)

GREEN

POSITIVE: Money, nature, peacefulness

NEGATIVE: Envy (the green monster); illness (he turned green)

PURPLE

POSITIVE: Royalty, spirituality, bravery (born to the purple, the Purple Heart)

NEGATIVE: Overly romantic or sentimental (purple prose), injury (bruising)

WHITE

POSITIVE: Purity (the white wedding gown); spirituality (white light)

NEGATIVE: Fear (he turned pale, ghostly); the color of mourning in many cultures

5"w × 7"h (12.5 × 18 cm), mixed-media collage on canvas

Feeling Happy, shows exuberance reflected through lime green and aqua.

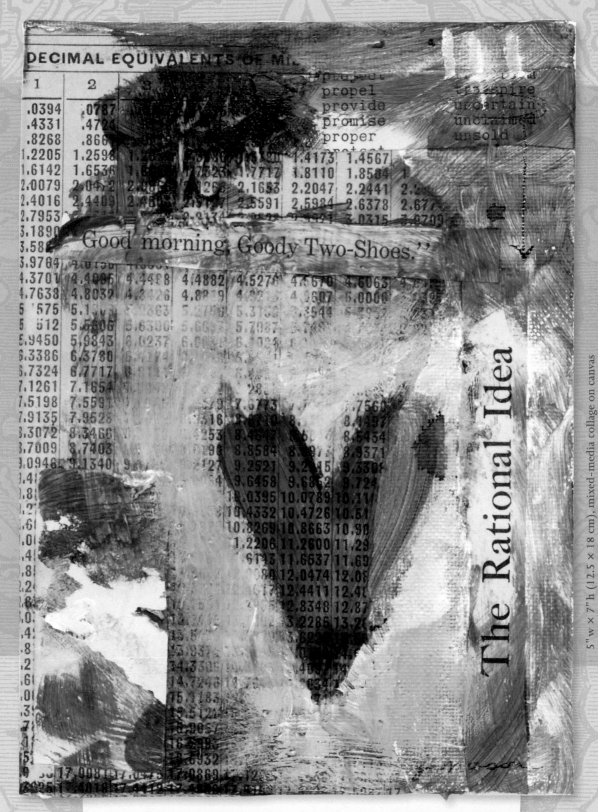

The Rational Idea

DECIMAL EQUIVALENTS OF MI...

"Good morning, Goody Two-Shoes."

propel
provide
promise
proper

transpire
uncertain
unclaimed
unsold

5"w × 7"h (12.5 × 18 cm), mixed-media collage on canvas

Feeling Rational, is a moody piece in which the artist describes that "being rational is not necessarily being happy, hence the blue."

who lives here? QUIZ

One of the best ways to uncover details about yourself is to study your surroundings. So get a pencil and paper, take a tour of your home, and answer the questions in this revealing quiz. When you find out who really lives in your house (that would be you, the way you really live), create a self-portrait that describes the "real" you. Note: there are no right or wrong answers. Just be open to what comes up and work with it. Meditate on your findings. Did you learn anything? Any surprises? Do you know yourself pretty well? It's all grist for the self-portrait mill.

WHAT KIND OF FURNITURE DO YOU OWN?

☐ Practically new. If the furniture is of your choosing, what style is it?

☐ Vintage/antique

☐ Contemporary

☐ Midcentury modern

☐ A lot of it is handmade, by you or other artist/crafters

☐ Dumpster Diva recycled pieces

☐ Ethnic-influenced

☐ Traditional

☐ An eclectic mix

☐ Shabby chic (stylish vintage)

☐ Early parent (hand-me-downs from Mom, Aunt Louise, and your second-to-last roommate—a mishmash)

☐ Currently someone else's (you still live at home, you moved into a prefurnished abode, you're living in a hotel, etc.)

LOOK AT YOUR BOOKSHELVES. WHAT OCCUPIES MOST OF THE SPACE?

☐ Nonfiction (If so, is there a theme?)

☐ Fantasy and/or sci-fi

☐ Romances

☐ Best sellers

☐ Mysteries

☐ Art and craft books

☐ Your journals

☐ Textbooks

☐ Art objects or pictures

☐ Empty space

Are the wall colors . . .

☐ Painted in deep or bright hues

☐ Painted all white

☐ Painted in pastels

☐ Wallpapered

☐ Painted or papered in whatever color they were when you moved in, and you haven't bothered to change them

☐ Painted or collaged with murals or some other artistic treatment

Are the rooms...

- ☐ In perfect order, with a place for everything

- ☐ A holy mess, with stuff scattered about seemingly at random

- ☐ Something in between: If your mom called and said she was coming over in twenty minutes, you could have the place in reasonable shape.

For accent pieces and wall decoration, do you mostly have . . .

- ☐ Pictures of family and friends

- ☐ Your own and others' artwork

- ☐ The kids' artwork

- ☐ Ethnic pieces you've collected on your travels

- ☐ Vintage pieces and found items you couldn't resist

- ☐ A mélange

- ☐ Something someone else picked out

- ☐ Nothing—you prefer the minimalist approach.

ARE THE MAGAZINES AND PERIODICALS MOSTLY...

- ☐ Art-related

- ☐ Home-related

- ☐ Parenting-related

- ☐ Political journals

- ☐ News-oriented

- ☐ Fashion-oriented

- ☐ Sport-oriented

- ☐ Stacked up, unread

LOOK IN YOUR FRIDGE AND KITCHEN CUPBOARDS. DO THEY CONTAIN . . .

- ☐ An epicurean's fantasy of hard-to-find delicacies

- ☐ The staples of a healthy eater

- ☐ The staples of a classic kitchen

- ☐ The staples of a single woman—yogurt, lettuce, white wine, and chocolate

- ☐ The staples of a single man—leftover pizza, condiments, beer, and chips

- ☐ Mom's or roommate's home cooking

- ☐ Take-out menus

DOES YOUR MEDICINE CHEST/BATH VANITY PRIMARILY CONTAIN . . .

- ☐ Cosmetics of every description

- ☐ Pharmaceuticals and first-aid supplies to cover every emergency

- ☐ Four kinds of toothpaste, all half-used

- ☐ Indulgent bath products

- ☐ The basics—soap, razor, toothpaste, toothbrush, moisturizer

On your front door there is a . . .

- ☐ Seasonal wreath or decorative sign

- ☐ Curtain

- ☐ Conservative paint color or stained wood

- ☐ Wild paint job signaling that an artist lives here

- ☐ Doorknob

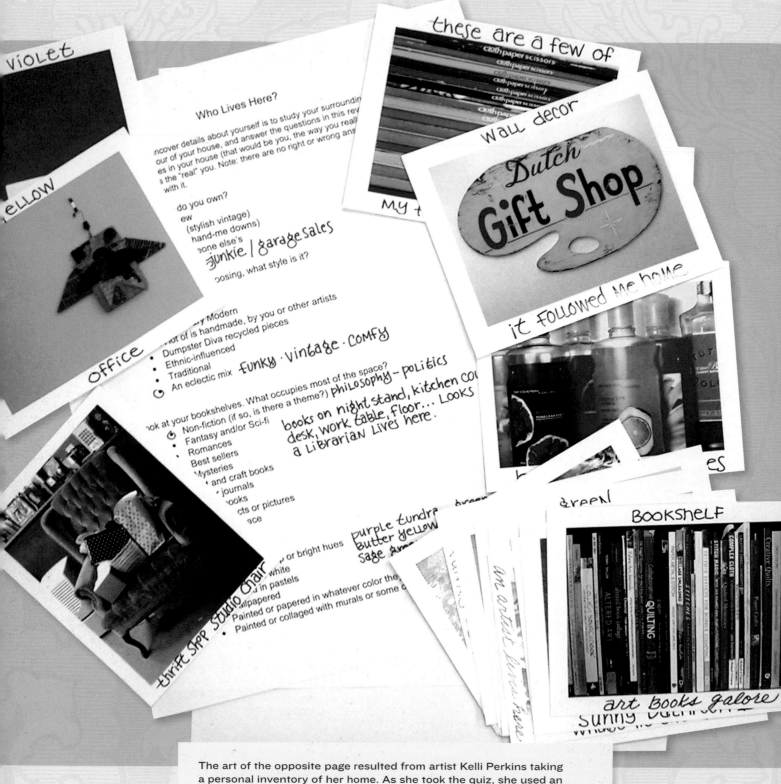

VIOLET

YELLOW

office

thrift shop Studio chair

these are a few of

wall decor

Dutch Gift Shop

it Followed me home

green

BOOKSHELF

art books galore

Who Lives Here?

ncover details about yourself is to study your surroundin
our of your house, and answer the questions in this rev
es in your house (that would be you, the way you real
s the "real" you. Note: there are no right or wrong an
with it.

do you own?
   ew
   (stylish vintage)
   hand-me downs)
   one else's
   junkie / garage sales

oosing, what style is it?

   Modern
   ot of is handmade, by you or other artists
   Dumpster Diva recycled pieces
   Ethnic-influenced
   Traditional
   An eclectic mix   Funky · vintage · comfy

ok at your bookshelves. What occupies most of the space?
   Non-fiction (if so, is there a theme?) philosophy - politics
   Fantasy and/or Sci-fi   books on night stand, kitchen co
   Romances   desk, work table, floor... Looks
   Best sellers   a Librarian Lives here.
   Mysteries
   and craft books
   journals
   ooks
   cts or pictures
   ce

purple tundra
butter yellow
sage

or bright hues
white
in pastels
allpapered
Painted or papered in whatever color the
Painted or collaged with murals or some

The art of the opposite page resulted from artist Kelli Perkins taking
a personal inventory of her home. As she took the quiz, she used an
instant camera to photograph objects around her home. She then used
the images as inspiration for a mixed-media collage that includes images,
fabric, and lots of texture.

11"w × 17"h (28 × 43 cm), mixed-media collage

"I based one of the postcards on my name, because I started my bio by stating my name and its origin. I've always loved that I was named after a character in a book and I love my name."

"The postcards with numbers are based on the zip codes of places I've lived. The whale is for the Upper West Side (Natural History Museum), which is my favorite place I've lived."

"This is my father in a photo booth shot. He wore a lot of plaid."

"HIGHLIGHTS" PORTRAIT

For this exercise, you'll need a timer and a word processor or pencil and notebook. Set the timer for ten minutes and then write your autobiography. Don't stop to think, don't worry about grammar or spelling, just write. When the timer goes off, stop. Don't edit. Now go back and highlight words, phrases, or sentences that jump out at you. Did you remember incidents that you had forgotten? Do you notice any patterns? Are there important aspects of your life missing? Use your findings to create a series of 4" × 6" postcard-size collages that tell the story of your life.

This series of postcards represents the highlights of artist Elin Waterson's life. Before she made the art, she wrote this short biography: "My name is Elin. I was named after a character in a children's book that my mother read to my sister Karen when she was pregnant with me. I was born in Pittsburgh Pennsylvania to my mother Nancy and my father Vince.

"We moved to Rowayton, Connecticut, when I was very young and then back to Pittsburgh. We lived in an old, renovated barn. I'm Scottish. I took a lot of dance classes my whole life, including highland dancing. We had lots of cats, which lived outside because my mother was allergic to them, and dogs that lived inside and out.

My mother was very artistic. We took art classes together when I was little. She always encouraged me to be creative. I went to college in Michigan and studied theater design (costume). After that I went to grad school, also for design. My favorite subject was art history - I like Pop Art and Fauvism. I worked in theater, film & television after I graduated. I met my husband David, a cinematographer, on a movie set. I moved to New York, we got married and had our son Lex. We lived in the West Village and then the Upper West Side (two blocks from the Natural History Museum, where I spent every Friday afternoon for years). Now we live in Westchester County, with our two little dogs. Lex is at RISD studying art, photography and filmmaking.

"I work at the Katonah Art Center as an art instructor and as Visual Arts Director. I also do freelance graphic design and web design work. I am a participating artist in the Art-o-mat program.

"I like to go see live music and stay out really late."

"CHOOSE A NEW ADVENTURE" PORTRAIT

Choose three photos of yourself—one from childhood, one from the middle of your life so far, and one that's current. Make up a story about each one that has nothing to do with your real life. Incorporate the picture and story into a collage, a la Chagall.

Artist Larissa Davis began this photo collage with a photo of herself when she was two years old in a rowboat with her father. Here is her commentary on the piece: "I noted that I was wearing pink, a color which I never wore after my early years," she said. "It made me think of my fascination with Cinderella, and the fantasy of being a beautiful princess who had the one aim in life of uniting with her perfect prince.

"The photo from my midlife at first did not speak to me, except that I recognized a rather sultry look on my face. That look led me down a path of reflection. At that time I fully rejected the princess fantasy and embraced real life experience and knowledge of the world around me and inside me. Ultimately this area of the collage, with me in meditation and me taking the apple from the tree, became the richest and most interesting to me.

"Given the story I was telling in the first 2 parts of the collage, I contemplated what story my last photo would tell. Many things have happened to me in the 20 years since the middle of my life, and one thing that came up clearly was that I have remade the early childhood fantasy into my real world. I wear an elaborate crown, and again wear the color pink. The castle has become my real home (the yellow farmhouse) and in the foreground are my 2 sons who swung into my life bringing new meaning, direction, and joy."

11"w × 17"h (28 × 43 cm), mixed-media collage

"CREATE A NEW IDENTITY" PORTRAIT

Have you ever noticed that when young schoolchildren draw a portrait of someone, whether the subject is a historical figure or just a Pilgrim or a princess, the face almost always resembles that of the child? Underneath the sweet innocence of this act is the fact that children have great imaginations, and they are imagining themselves, however subconsciously, as the person they are drawing.

So try it yourself. Imagine yourself as an ancestor from a different time and place, a person who lives in a completely different country or culture, or as a famous icon (Marilyn Monroe, Botticelli's Venus, James Dean) and create a self-portrait based on the idea. Be sure to take notes and keep track of your reactions and discoveries.

TRY THESE IDEAS

✦ Dress up as the "character" and photograph yourself. If you never wear makeup, get glam. If you normally dress in trendy clothes and wild colors, make yourself over in classic Grace Kelly fashion or as a prim schoolmarm.

✦ Find an existing image of the type of person or the celebrity you wish to emulate and alter it digitally with your face and/or body.

✦ Put yourself in the setting. Use a photo of yourself or draw yourself in an imagined setting—on a pirate ship, in an eighteenth-century salon, or strolling along the Nile in ancient times.

✦ Re-create a famous work of art, such as *The Mona Lisa* or Rembrandt's *The Night Watch*, but include symbolism from your own life.

✦ Select a photo of yourself, past or current, and use pens, markers, fabric, paint, etc., to change the pictures to show an altered version of you in that world—for example, what you should have been, what you're really thinking, or what you aspire to be.

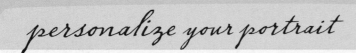

personalize your portrait

Here are some ways to infuse your self-portrait with little bits of you:

✦ Handprints or fingerprints

✦ A silhouette of your profile

✦ Your handwriting

✦ Copies of ephemera, such as your birth certificate or stamped pages from your passport

✦ Poems you wrote or pictures you drew as a child

✦ Your personal symbol

✦ A favorite saying, motto, or sign-off

✦ Photographs of your ancestors

✦ Your family crest (inherited or imagined)

✦ Your shadow

✦ A rubbing of your license plate or other embossed emblem

✦ Your initials

✦ The names of your children, pets, or other family members

Your Life Is Your Work of Art

MATTER AND MIND

11" w. × 17" h. (28 × 43 cm), altered photo and collage
K. Michel 2005

"Almost always it is the fear of being ourselves that brings us to the mirror."
—Antonio Porchia, *Voces*, 1943,
translated from *Spanish* by W. S. Merwin

Artist Karen Michel altered this photo of herself to hyper-emphasize her feelings while collecting treasures on the beach. "I tend to collect feathers, so I am presenting my found 'loot.' I feel it exhibits my love for the natural world, showing that it is where my heart shines the brightest."

SELF-PORTRAIT *exercises*

When, as a child, we first get enough muscle control and brain power to draw a shape beyond a scribble, we often draw faces. It makes sense, since we've been staring into other people's faces and learning the words "eyes," "nose," and "mouth" from infancy. But in fact, drawing a specific likeness can be very difficult for most of us. How to position the features so they are in proportion? How to draw the eyes so that they look like they're really seeing, with the depth that truly makes them the mirrors of the soul? The following exercises will give you techniques for getting familiar with faces, drawing caricatures, and focusing on the all-important eyes.

proportions of human anatomy

Use these guidelines when rendering the human form, whether you plan the results to be proportionate or not.

HEIGHT The human figure is an average of seven heads high.

TORSO The distance from the top of the head to the bottom of the chest is two heads.

BUTTOCKS The length from the top to the bottom of the buttocks is one head.

LEG LENGTH The distance from the hip to the toes is four heads.

WINGSPAN The width from shoulder to shoulder is three heads' width.

FOREARM The distance from the elbow to the end of the outstretched fingers is two heads.

GIRTH OF HAND The distance from the wrist to the end of the outstretched fingers of the hand is one head.

MIRROR MIRROR
By Kelli Perkins

This exercise gives you a simple tool for drawing your own face while at the same time revealing information about your face's shape and its features that can be helpful in future portraits. What you see as you draw may be very different from what you "see" when you look in the mirror or at a photograph. Are the eyes located in the top third of the face or more toward the center? How does your hairline shape your face? How can you capture the shape of your nose? If you do the exercise a second time, does anything change? Studying your face in this way can help you be more objective about your looks, moving you beyond self-consciousness into self-portraiture.

drawing a SELF-PORTRAIT

1   Find a mirror in your house to which you can get close or set up a mirror on a table. You must be able to see your whole face in the mirror. You should be no more than a few inches away so that your complexion is large enough to work with. Settle into a chair and find something to act as an armrest so your body can remain still while you draw.

2   Securely tape a transparency sheet to the mirror where your face is reflected. Close one eye and keep it closed throughout this process. With a fine permanent marker, dot the transparency where one of your nostrils is so you can keep your head lined up with it while you work. You will need to constantly readjust to this dot as your eye moves away from the dot to follow the lines you are drawing.

   With the marker, trace your face and hair and outline your individual features. Finish with your shoulders and neckline. Don't be discouraged if your first attempt is not successful. Try different lighting and experiment with your proximity to the mirror. Have extra transparencies on hand with which to work.

MATERIALS

- Transparency sheets • Mirror
- Masking tape • Permanent marker
- Chair

Practice drawing your image on a transparency until you get a feel for the shape of your face and proportions of your features.

3 Remove the transparency from the mirror and look at it. Note some essential things about your face. What is its basic shape? Is it round, oval, or square? What is the shape of your hair? Look at the placement of your eyes—do they sit high on your face or low? What is the shape of your nose? Look at your mouth—is one lip bigger than the other? What is the arch of your eyebrows? Compare your face with other faces to get a sense of how your features are uniquely arranged. Take a medium-point marker and go over the fine lines to even them out and make your portrait bolder.

4 Turn the transparency over so that you are no longer looking at your mirror image; you are observing your face the same way another person who is facing you does. I thought my self-portraits were out of whack until someone reminded me that mirror images are reversed! Tape the transparency to a window with a piece of drawing paper on top of it. Use the mirror drawing to sketch your face. Try drawing it in a single line or two and repeat until you get a feeling for the proportions of your face.

Once you are satisfied with a drawing, outline it with a medium-point permanent marker to give it definition.

In this caricature, Kelli emphasized her mouth and glasses and added color to her hair. All allude to her vibrancy and zest for life.

"What are the elements that allow people to recognize you as you? These observations will determine which features should be emphasized by playing with proportion."

—Kelli

CARICATURES

Once you have mastered the basics of your countenance, it's time to have some fun with caricatures. A caricature is a portrait that exaggerates prominent features (or personality traits—like a big mouth on someone known to talk a lot) while retaining the likeness of the person portrayed. Drawing caricatures helps sharpen your powers of observation. Because some of the features are exaggerated, this kind of portrait has a point of view or tells a story about the subject. This technique therefore teaches you a way to imbue your self-portrait with personality and meaning while also honing your drawing skills.

The hallmark of a caricature is simple, bold lines you can draw with confidence. So practice drawing your features on scrap paper until you can capture them in one pen stroke. If it helps, use grid paper to establish size and placement. Once you've mastered a personal caricature, you've taken another step toward making your unique mark on the world.

Step back and look at your face to determine which features are larger or smaller compared to your overall face. What are the elements that allow people to recognize you as you? These observations will determine which features should be emphasized by playing with proportion. Does your mouth turn up or down? Is your nose proportional, too big, or is it a small button nose? You can also exaggerate the shape of your face, the height of your hair, or the size of your glasses or teeth.

DIGITAL *self-portraits*
By Kimberly Montagnese

A photograph, rather than a rendering of yourself, can also be the basis of your mixed-media self-portrait. Your digital camera is a great tool for capturing your image. Once satisfied with an image, upload it to your computer and start to play! You can digitally alter your image in an almost overwhelming number of ways (for more on digital techniques, please see pages 16–25).

Digital images of yourself can be altered in any number of ways. For this piece, Kimberly removed all of the color from the image, pumped up the contrast and then combined cutouts of the image with sewing and fabric. See the following page for detailed instructions.

9"w × 12"h (23 × 31 cm)
Mixed-media photo with collage stitch

using a **DIGITAL IMAGE WITH FABRIC**

1 Soften the black paint with water. Paint one sheet of Yupo with the black paint. Leave some streaks and add water to make it mottled. Allow it to dry and then spray it with clear lacquer to seal the color.

2 Using image-editing software, convert the image to gray scale. Adjust the contrast and shadow as well as color until you achieve your desired effect. Print the image onto another sheet of Yupo. Seal the ink with a couple coats of clear lacquer.

3 Using a craft knife, cut away all the white portions of the photo, leaving only the black and gray areas.

4 Apply fusible web to the back of the fabric and fuse the fabric onto the Timtex.

5 Position the cutout photo on the fabric side of the Timtex. Secure the photo in place by sewing through the photo and Timtex with the monofilament thread.

6 On the larger, painted Yupo, use the craft knife to cut a 5" × 7" opening (tilted angle) in the lower corner. Place the stitched photo behind the opening. Stitch around the outside edges of the "frame" with the monofilament thread.

7 Use the leftover bits of fused fabric and Timtex to create small squares. Glue them in place, then stitch.

8 Apply glue to the back of the finished piece. Press a piece of heavy kraft paper over the back. Press in place and then sew around the outside edges.

9 Trim away the excess paper.

10 To prevent warping, place heavy books on top of the piece until the glue dries.

MATERIALS

Yupo translucent watercolor paper • Black Prang professional watercolor paint • Water • Clear, high-gloss spray lacquer • Digital or scanned photo of yourself • Ink-jet printer • Image-editing software • Hand-dyed or commercial fabric (6" × 8") • Wonder-Under fusible web • Timtex stabilizer (6" × 8") • YLI smoky monofilament thread • Glue stick • Craft knife • Kraft paper

This piece was also altered digitally. After the photo was converted to black and white, text was overlaid on top if it. Cropped portions of the text dot the background to create a contemporary corner frame.

9"w × 12"h (23 × 31 cm)
Mixed-media photo with collage stitch

FOCUS on the eyes
By Carol Kemp

The symbol that has always shown up in the corners of my notebooks in school and the scratch paper by my phone has been the eye. I suppose because the eyes tell so much about living beings. As an artist, the symbol continues in my work, but there is also my desire to understand the eye and the face in which it sits. In August of 2006, I challenged myself to create and post a face a day in a blog. The visage could come from my mind, an observation, or a photograph. The boundaries were very wide, and I could use any medium and subject that had a face. I did this for one year and surprisingly used my own face fewer than 20 times out of 365 postings. However, this experiment taught me a lot about portraiture and self-portraits, as well as the experience of making art every day.

In these examples I am using watercolor, but the ideas hold true as to form and shape with any medium. Look at your own eyes while reading this discussion to strengthen your observation.

THE EYELID AND MUSCLE

The eyes are not shaped like footballs, but rather are balls covered by a slit in the skin, which, when opened, has the shape of a football or almond. The slit has a thickness, and that knowledge helps to make an eye look more three-dimensional. Also, when the eye is opened, a crease (or two or more) is created as the skin sits on top and around the eyeball. At the corner of the eye is a muscle, one of many that allow movement of the eye. This is the area that collects the sleep sand. Including that little pink muscle will help create depth. Because there is a thickness of skin around the eye, a shadow is created above the eye.

In the steps on the right, Carol explains in detail how to capture depth and vitality when drawing one's own set of eyes.

11"w × 17"h (28 × 43 cm)

THE IRIS

The iris of the eye is not seen as a complete circle unless the person is in a pose of surprise; keep that in mind when drawing the iris. Some artists paint the "whites" of the eyes first, leaving the iris as negative space to be filled in. This technique works well with acrylic, oils, and pastels. Note that the iris is a color or combination of colors (take a look in the mirror) and the pupil is black.

THE TWINKLE

The last important step is the reflection of light, or what I call the "spark of life." That reflection, done with a dash of white (or absence of paint with watercolor) is what gives the eye "life."

drawing MY EYES

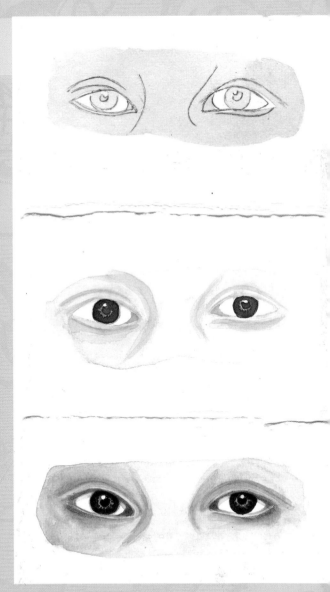

1 First, I used a pencil to draw lines to represent the shapes and creases of my eye, including the shape of the reflective light that shines on the iris and pupil. I traced the pencil lines with a kneaded eraser to lessen the graphite marks. I created a light wash of light pink and yellow and a tiny bit of blue to create an underlying skin tone. This is a subjective choice that can be played with to create the skin tone you desire. I covered the whole drawing with this wash, except the whites of the eyes and the reflective spot.

2 Once dry, I began to color the iris and pupil. I have blue eyes, so I built up the color of my eye, layer by layer. To capture the nuances in my eye color, I used layers of washes rather than applying one thick coat of color. Also, while waiting for the paint to dry in the iris, I applied washes of rose and yellow with a bit of blue over the deepest crease lines above and below the eye as well as to the side of the nose, deepening the shadow that is created by the bridge of the nose. I also darkened the muscle area at the corner of the eye.

Though I continued to darken these areas to create the form of the eye, I tried to avoid putting any of this wash above and below the iris along the rim below the eye. I wanted to maintain a lighter value here to help create the roundness of the form.

3 Once the washes were dry, using the very small point of my brush, I lightly outlined the eyelid and the under rim. I wanted this to be a very subtle line, so I was careful with the amount of moisture on my brush. Also, at this point, I added black to the pupil of the eye. The upper lid of the eye created a shadow. This shadow was generated using a light wash of gray made by mixing blue into my orange-ish pink wash I had been using. This was one of the last things I did because my painting had to be dry or it would have smudged. I have very little color in my eyelashes, so I showed them as just a touch of shadow. You will need to add more shadow for darker lashes, but take care; a few subtle wisps of lash go a long way.

PLACING THE EYES INTO CONTEXT

Recently, some friends came by my studio and, observing the many self-portraits I had made, commented that each portrait represented an aspect of me, a part of my whole. It was an affirming moment and I realized the truth of that statement. The self-portrait is another glimpse into the complexity of one's personality and its purpose is not one of physical identification, like a driver's license, but rather a view of one of the facets of oneself, one of many that make up the multifaceted beings that we are.

example 1

ERASED CHARCOAL I began by drawing, using an eraser as my drawing tool. I covered a piece of charcoal paper with a thick coat of charcoal and began to remove the light areas with a kneaded eraser. This is an excellent exercise in seeing the shapes of shadows. The outcome is called *chiaroscuro*, which literally means "light-dark" and was skillfully employed by Leonardo da Vinci, Rembrandt, and Caravaggio. I love the effect, though my intention to hold the pose gives the portrait a very severe look. I collaged some old book pages on one side, washed the paper with gesso, and wrote some positive affirmations with red pastel pencil.

11"w × 17"h (28 × 43 cm)

example 2

GRAPHITE I used a Polaroid photo I took of myself as the reference. I again began with a contour warm-up on heavyweight watercolor paper. I created a continuous shaded portrait in graphite, using the contour lines as my guide. Although I like the graphite drawing on its own, I enjoy color more, so I laid down washes of watercolor. For the background, I lightly drew in a design and carefully covered the negative space of the design with rubbings from a white candle. The wax acts as a resist, so when I watercolored purple over the background, the leaf design was filled in with a batik effect behind it. I then went over the background with an iron to remove the wax (after covering it with a paper towel to soak up the wax as it melts) and washed over the whole thing with quinacridone burnt orange. Even with the purple batik background, the softness of the watercolors around my face and the graphite lines and shading emphasize my blue eyes all the more.

11"w × 17"h (28 × 43 cm)

example 3

MONOTYPE Monotypes can be made with various media, but for this I used water-soluble oil pastels. The plate is an extruded acrylic panel and after completing my drawing on it, I placed a sheet of heavy-weight watercolor paper that was moistened with water on top. I burnished the paper with my hands, pulling up the corners to check if the image was printing. The finished print has bold and intense colors, as I tend to be a bit of a fauve. Exaggerating the features, especially the eyes, adds to this effect.

11"w × 17"h (28 × 43 cm)

example 4

ACRYLIC I began by finding the shapes of my face, constantly gauging the distances of features and proportions. I used a light wash to draw in the shapes, the side of my face, and placement of the eyes, nose, mouth, and the neck and hairline. I tend to use an unrealistic color scheme, one that leans toward warm colors, but for this one I used a lot of purple. The eyes are large, not unusual for me as I place a lot of importance on them, but I was frustrated with the mouth. I made myself look so old. Later, I decided to approach this portrait from a different angle. I made photocopies of it as well as two other portraits and ripped them up, taking one eye from one painting, one from another, and the nose and mouth from another. I collaged these onto a mat board that I primed with gesso, front and back, and painted over them with a pink glaze, redrawing the hair, neck, and shoulders with conté crayon and chalk pastels. I added some of my favorite symbols to the background and collaged in some origami papers. The spirals and circles represent the feminine aspect as well as the growth potential in life. The color purple is for spirituality, which is very important to me. I was trying to create the feeling of festive exuberance, which is how I feel about my life, especially when I am "in the zone" while creating.

The painting above and center is a collage of three different self-portraits. The eyes for this piece were taken from the pieces on either side of the middle portrait.

11"w × 17"h (28 × 43 cm) each

GETTING *started*

So far you've done some self-assessment, sketched, and studied your eyes and face. Now it's time to start pulling these elements together. But where to begin? The next two essays take you through the artist's creative process, from inspiration for the big picture through choosing the smaller elements that you will incorporate into a self-portrait collage. As these artists show, your first step along the path to a self-portrait can be through meditation, journaling, flipping through art books, photographs of yourself, a funny turn of phrase, your own name, the results of the exercises you did at the beginning of this chapter, or something you came up with on your own. There is no right or wrong, just experimentation, practice, and—if you banish your inner critic—a lot of fun.

JUMP-STARTING *your work*
By Katie Kendrick

I consider all the artwork I create a self-portrait in one form or another, whether it's a painting, a doll, or an assemblage. I find creating visual art to be the most powerful way for me to connect to my feelings, my heart, and my intuition—to the dynamic flow of the universe. It's an effective way in which I can align with myself when I'm out of touch, like an adjustment from a universal psychic chiropractor. The act of putting down paint and pencil lines, cutting and gluing scraps of paper, and sewing bits and pieces of fabric together touches those places inside me that need

to see the light of day, that might need healing, or that just need to be shared with another living soul. Many times I don't know what it is I want to express, what I'm longing to understand, or even where to begin. Typically, I won't fully understand what it is my artwork is communicating to me for several hours or sometimes even days or weeks. In this way, my art reflects the mystery I am, even to my own self, and by staying true to myself as I create, I honor that truth. The following method is one I sometimes use to get jump started, and once going, to dig deeper.

STAGE 1:
find inspiration

+ Pull out my favorite art books. (I have several books of artwork by Chagall, as I feel an affinity toward his work.) Grab books with portrait photography. Thumb through pages until something speaks—use of color, content, a facial expression.

+ Decipher the elements in said piece. Hmm, is it the tilt of a head or body, the size and placement of the eyes, the colors and shadows, or maybe it's the overall tone of the piece? Depends on mood. . . . Take note of mood and wonder how it is affecting my thought process.

+ Begin to translate elements into my own artistic language of color and form. DO NOT DUPLICATE OR IMITATE! Well, try, anyway.

+ Interact with myself in the mirror. Take this opportunity to notice distinct parts of myself, like my rosy cheeks, my graying hair, my mother's hands, or the uncertainty reflected in my eyes.

STAGE 2:
prime the canvas

+ Apply a few of coats of gesso to watercolor paper.

+ Study the canvas. Too empty? Glue down a few collage elements—a phone book page, part of an old letter, any scraps of paper. YES! A piece of vinyl wallpaper also makes a good painting surface—it's extremely tough and stands up to rigorous sanding, layering, and most any kind of abuse an artist can dish out.

+ Apply a couple light coats of gesso over the wallpaper, allowing some of the patterned areas to show through.

"In this piece, *My Guardian Angel*, wonder and curiosity are reflected in these big eyes, as well as a sense of faith that everything will work out, and work toward good, regardless of how things seem," artist Katie Kendrick says. "My guardian angel is my constant companion, always there watching over me, comforting me, and keeping watch over my soul amidst all my busy comings and goings."

7"w × 10"h (18 × 25 cm)
Paint and mixed media

STAGE 3:
start creating

✦ Lay down some lines and shapes with pencil, rubbing out or drawing over areas that don't feel right.

✦ Add color with acrylic paint, watercolor crayons, or oil pastels.

✦ Note: Nothing looks like much of anything. Relax. It's not supposed to. Remind self: You've just begun, and this is playtime.

✦ Put inspirational piece aside . . . I am well on my way, my own way, and I have plenty of inspiration inside.

STAGE 4:
self-awareness

✦ What is percolating under the skin as I work? Why am I creating angular/organic/soft shapes? How are my color choices making me feel? How is this layering business affecting me?

✦ Tension check: Am I relaxed? Am I open? Or am I closed, tense, and uncomfortable?

✦ I am closed and tense. I have a most unwelcome guest in my mind: The Critic.

✦ Open door to mind, cordially show her out, and while the door is open, invite in the breeze, the sunshine, and all that is refreshing to my mind and spirit.

> "Thoughts are potent, and criticism poisons the creative process; instead of placing judgment, why not invite the dynamic emptiness to reside in you instead, the place where all creation is birthed of mystery."
> —Katie

11"w × 14"h (20 × 36 cm), paint and mixed media

"*A Daily Visitor* was inspired by the natural beauty that surrounds my life and home here near the woods and river," Katie says. "The piece of wood was one I found at the water's edge. I began by drawing the face with my non-dominant hand, then painting it and then the background. Once those were completed, I had a clear idea of how the body needed to be and which other elements were needed."

11" w × 14"h (20 × 36 cm), paint and mixed media

✦ Hello, materials! How do you do? Let's play!

✦ Be curious and encourage my "I wonder what will happen if I do this?" attitude.

✦ Be as daring as a trapeze artist.

✦ Be vigilant with my thoughts; be awake and aware as I create, check in with myself often. There is plenty of room for all of my feelings and sensations. Be an observer; record my observations with my hands, the paint, and the medium.

✦ Avoid understanding. Understanding and any judgment of that which is arising as I create is unnecessary and often undesirable—it can easily obstruct the dynamic flow.

creating mood through material

The materials you use will no doubt affect the mood and tone of your art. Here are some guidelines to use when considering them:

To evoke softness and comfort
Velvet and other napped fabrics • Fake fur • Worn vintage fabrics • Chalk pastels • Embroidery • Old handwritten recipes and cookbook pages • Wood

To suggest childhood and memories
Old school papers, such as kindergarten writing samples • Saved letters • Vintage photographs • Watercolors • Aging products like patina solutions and walnut ink • Copyright-free images and text from school primers and children's books • Small found objects like toys and trinkets

To convey a contemporary feeling
Heavy-bodied acrylic paints • Grids • Plastic mesh fencing • Geometric or color-block printed fabric • Clean metal hardware • Used computer/electronic parts • Rubber stamps with abstract designs • Enamel finishes

WHERE DO THOSE *ideas come from?*

By Yvonne Porcella

People often ask me how I get the ideas for my self-portrait quilts. Normally there's a flood, and I have to have the presence of mind to capture the ideas as they stream from my mind. Take the theme for *Chasing the Purple Dog*, the quilt shown at right. I had just visited Sioux City, Iowa, and learned the word for snake in the Dakota language is "sioux," so I just had to use a snake in my next quilt. Just as I am deep into thought about my snake, our dog comes into the studio, barking to be taken outside.

Often a break from the concentration of the studio gives me time to think about different images, and this can take my work in another direction. From an import shop, I purchased a small carved wooden dog that succumbed to a termite infestation. It is a symbol I have used in many quilts, in large format and small, in purple fabric and in black-and-white check fabric.

A trip to Santa Fe, New Mexico, generated the idea to use chili peppers as a design shape. Red and green chilies, along with the purple dog, have been stitched together in several of my large quilts. One day when I was having lunch at La Fonda, the famous hotel in the heart of Santa Fe, the waitress offered four choices to my simple request for a taco: "Yellow or blue corn tortilla, red or green chili sauce?" That simple question set up a whole chain of ideas that found their way into my quilts.

Fast-forward to a studio visit by a small quilting group. One of the women saw a series of six large portrait quilts on my wall. She turned to me and stated that I must have terrible nightmares. Then she asked where I get my ideas. I frankly told her that I have lots of ideas; they rattle around in my head, and when I stand over my worktable, the designs just drip out of my nose. For the theme of *Head Trip*, the design concept was to use food to illustrate part of my persona. Thoughts of how hot that green chili was and how much I prefer red chili led to thoughts of how eating the wrong type of red chilies really does make your nose run.

Now that I have my design for my nose, the rest of the head follows from scraps and images I like. I have just a small fragment of fabric printed like jigsaw puzzle pieces; it fit perfectly onto the tip of the chili pepper. My favorite childhood flower is the calla lily. They grew in everyone's garden where I lived. Black-and-white prints are a favorite, as are checks in any color combination. I like hearts and stars, flowers, leaves, ice cream cones, polka dots. A bit of rock-print fabric is on hand for that famous idea of one "having rocks in her head." I also like to note how ideas are sorted in, or enter, my head, either using a symbol of a windup key or an arrow.

As for the "Y," a few years ago I dropped off some film to be developed and the young man behind the counter asked for my last name; I responded, "Porcella." He asked for my first initial; I responded, "Y." He answered, "because we need it." At first disgruntled, I was able to turn this episode into a wonderful hidden—but now revealed—design concept. The question mark is, for me, a symbolic Y and the P is hidden somewhere in the design.

This self-portrait quilt is a wonderful example of how ideas flowing stream-of-consciousness can turn into very personal art.

12"w × 12"h (31 × 31 cm)
Cotton, silks, fused fabrics, machine-quilted, hand-beaded, fabric paint

WORKING through it

It's entirely possible that tomorrow you will sit down in the morning to make a self-portrait and be done well before lunch. Possible, but unlikely. In fact, self-portraits are a lot like the people who make them: a work in progress. When you begin, you'll feel inspired and have a lot of great ideas. Some will work, and some won't. You may try to force the concept you started with, ignoring the little voice that's telling you to try something else. Listen to the voice. If you're still getting nowhere, walk away. When you come back, you'll have a fresh perspective. You may even have the courage to tear up what you've done so far and start again, if that's what's necessary. Or you may find that like life, it's the process that counts, not necessarily the result.

SELF-PORTRAIT sketchbook meanderings
By Donna Anderson

Mixed-media artist Donna Anderson thought it might be fun—and a stretch of her considerable imagination—to make a self-portrait in the abstract style. She particularly wanted to explore cubism. She kept a journal as she worked through this creative exercise, and here it is, just as she wrote it.

8 30 07
Your eye will fill in what is missing . . . .
Everything is not needed . . . .
Open space rests the eye . . .

Rest.

Don't fill in everything! White space. Hard & soft lines.

I am studying cubism for a future painting . . . . While working on the self-portrait for MMSP book, may achieve the cubist effect in mixed media.

3 photos of myself that might be usable. Bring them into Photoshop 2

Play.
Distort image.
Sphere twirl.
Diffused glow WOW Ghostly. . . I'll do a vampire version! What fun!

09 02 07

Not sure where to begin. . . Don't feel like I got very far the 1st day. I don't like this stage. feels unproductive. . . . but necessary.

Research internet for abstract portraits.

PICASSO of course is the most prominent. I also love Lich-tenstein.
Clean lines.

Photoshop again.
Bringing photos into Filter effects . . playing . . noise, cut out, distort . . looking for organic shapes to distort. So I must break the photo down to the most important shapes & not lose the soul of the face.

Okay . . not getting anywhere . . .
Printed out 8 ½ X 11 picture of myself that has been cropped enlarged.

LITE TABLE fun! Love the light table. (Fun to use at night in my studio. . . . like a secret.)

Trace image loosely & incomplete. Shift tracing paper on other areas & trace. (Ex. Cutting in 1/2 vertically sliding image or choosing a different image to combine to make a full face .. then of course take part away. . . . DON'T need the whole face.

Okay . . . finally . . . a very productive day.

When artist Donna Anderson began working on this project, she first selected several possible images with which to work. On the pages that follow, you will see several of her beginning sketches and read the reasons why she liked and/or disliked the results.

09 03 07

Reduce parts to organic shapes & mix w/realistic imagery.

More Photoshop . . . I could do this all day.

Studying cubism for painting . . . . . translate into fabric . . . . not as easy as it seems!

Cut out square format sketch graphic paper . . . cut out square smaller than needed to fit on top of several sketches. Make a die-cut square for cropping.

09 06 07

I feel very lost. Just keep changing & shifting images on Photoshop & by hand . . . not happy w/any.

Do WE EVER like our own image?

Perhaps I should just sew some . . . I'll make a quick doll dress

The above sketch shows Donna's clearest attempt at cubism. Organic shapes were transformed into more geometric shapes. In the end, she felt it was too much of an imitation of Picasso, so she discarded it.

The two faces on this sketch represent Donna's different sides. She deconstructed the image into geometric shapes, leaving the hair in a more organic form. "I like the images separately, but not together," she says. "Here, they look cheesy, as if I were trying to create a mural."

This combination of photo and sketch illustrates how Donna experimented with parts of photos and images.

09 07 07

The 1st self-portrait for the QA challenge was so plain . . . I can see how I have grown. It was fun but boring.

I guess this is why I have mixed-media block. . . .

Okay . . . lets just DO IT! Mess'n around too much . . .
begin & it will come . . . no more mess'n on the computer . . . not going to be happy with any-thing . . . just do it.

1.   Photo enlarged
2.   light table
3.   extract some of the main lines

I prayed for guts 2 begin . . . this immediately came to me. Just take the 1st picture, the funky drawing, use different mediums/plastic, fiber & fibers.

Papers are everywhere . . . . . JUST BEGIN . . . . . gosh

09 10 07

I'm stil l / / / / / / / play'n. need to establish image size & placement.

Bigger . . . smaller . . . cropped?
Where are my organic shapes? . . .

lets forget the painting for a bit . . .
maybe that is what is confusing me . . .
need to concentrate on one medium.

Enlarged my head . . . it looks huge . . . the nose is a good thing to make a bit smaller!
but I think this is the best format . . . I will do 3 different ones. Once I get on a roll it will go quickly. Just pick one.

Eyes are the windows to the soul.

IT IS SO HARD TO LOOK @ MYSELF!

09 11 07

Oh just opened a Frappuccino . . . that will get me going.

Do not mess with any images on the computer until the final image has been chosen . . . then . . . playing time does not feel so wasted.

The cubism theme . . . I do not seem to be able to do this . . . I am determined but maybe not for this project.

Be still before God & pray for wisdom.

Okay . . . I have again decided on the image.
The 1st one will be a thread painting, basically . . . the medium I am most familiar with. Move to sculpty liquid etc.

1st Lutradur on fabric & found objects . . . Beginning with the easiest.
(I usually do the hardest things 1st to get them out of the way . . . but I must get on a roll & be secure in order to tackle the harder image.)

I want blue. Photoshop, reduce image to very pale. Just enough to see when mounted on fabric.

Audition fabric possibilities, just laying the image on the fabric . . . how much of the design shows through? Need more of a tone on tone . . . sometimes I feel like that is cheating. It takes away some of the difficulty & I like to solve those problems.

(Perhaps that is why I do not use the many purchased images I have in my possession.)

Okay . . . narrowed down to 3, one for each piece. Now I'm so excited & WANT to keep working but my role has changed to mommy . . . talk to you tomorrow.

09 12 07

NOW WE'RE HAV'N FUN!
Printed image on Lutradur, trim out (Melt)
with Walnut Hollow Textile tool. Layout on
chosen blue batik. Found-fabric swatches &
fun objects laid out in possible design.

Cut background fabric to correct size. Lay
Lutradur face & quilting pieces. Spray glue
parts down, now sew them to background.
Just enough to stay in place.

Play with all your doodads. Possibilities for
hair are limitless!

Thread painting
tv parts
beads
mohair (I was recently making a waldorf
doll . . . her hair was perfect, she let me
have a bit)
Schnauzer hair!
angelina in red, & blue
safety pens
springs
sequins
oil paint sticks
I'm sure I'm missing something . . but
that will do.

Remove all fun things, draw the face in
with a pencil or if going to be part of the
piece, black skinny marker.

Thread painting 1st, add all the good stuff,
decide on a binding.
I choose to leave part of the image w/o a
full frame.

After reading the journal entries from this artist,
you can see that she made several sketches
before beginning to construct the self-portrait
above. Not satisfied with any of the drawings,
she stopped sketching, settled on a straightfor-
ward approach, and started working with her
creative materials. She says if she could do it all
over again, she would take a different approach.

9½"w × 9½"h (24 × 24 cm)
Art quilt with mixed media

In self I trust

reveal yourself

WARMED UP? Feeling comfortable with yourself? Got your art supplies ready? It's time to delve into some more elaborate, finished, mixed-media self-portraits. The beauty of mixing media to make a self-portrait is that you have so many different techniques and textures on your palette with which to express the real you. After all, you are not one-dimensional, why should your art be?

In this chapter, we'll show you ways to visually explore and explain yourself through art dolls, collage, photography, a fabric book, a plaster cloth mask, an assemblage of found objects, and a photographic art quilt. Each of these projects comes with complete instructions, but they are just a way to get you started. As self-portraits are about self-expression, you should feel free to adapt or change any elements you choose—and certainly to come up with ideas of your own.

> "Thus a characterization is the mask which hides the actor-individual. Protected by it he can lay bare his soul down to the last intimate detail."
>
> —KONSTANTIN STANISLAVSKI

exploring ROLES

In society, at work, in our families, we are often defined by our roles. Man, woman, parent, accountant, artist, nurturer, enforcer, adventurer, jester—we all play many roles in the course of our lives, and often in the same day. Self-portraits are a way to explore and express (and vice versa), through dolls, dress-up, the written word, or the camera lens. By experimenting with the many different roles we play, we can help ourselves define or redefine them. Discover new ones and discard old ones. Ultimately, using self-portraits to explore our roles can lead to a greater understanding of ourselves.

self-discovery THROUGH JOURNAL DOLLS By Kelli Perkins

Doll play is a universal human custom and often the first step toward seeing ourselves as unique individuals. As a little girl, my dolls taught me much about the roles I would play later in life. They were every dream and every role I ever envisioned for myself. Through my cloth and plastic selves, I learned what a mom does, what a wife does, what a boss does, and what it means to be part of a community.

During the course of our lives, we change roles many times as we participate in an ongoing process of discovery and re-creation. There is no end to the ways in which we might express ourselves next. Creating a journal doll is an opportunity to evaluate our unique place in life and journal our feelings about the roles that give form to our presence. A journal doll is who we are and who we want to be. It's a love letter to ourselves. It can be based on a physical likeness or it may represent the inner narrative deep within us. Developing a personal iconography through role exploration can illuminate new paths for your art and ultimately your life.

BEGIN WITH A SELF-ASSESSMENT

In order to create a journal doll of your own, you'll need to start with a bit of discovery, so grab a pencil and paper and take a self-assessment.

+ Jot down words that describe your characteristics, such as "colorful," "smart," or "imaginative."

+ List functions that you perform at home, at work, and in your leisure time—cooking, mediating, or painting. Imagine that you had a name tag at different times of day when you are doing these tasks. What would that tag say?

CONSIDER YOUR ALTERNATE SELVES

You are multidimensional, so it will probably take more than one doll to express your personality.

+ Name your alter egos. If you had to "tag" yourself, what would you choose? How would others choose to tag you?

+ Pick the tags you think are most important and make them column headers. Take the words you wrote down to describe yourself and your functions and group them under the tags.

+ Walk yourself through your day and visualize all the things you do in this role, adding role words.

+ Create a list of physical symbols to represent these traits. For "mother," you might include "nest," "blanket," "spoon," "heart," "home," etc.

+ Use these visual cues to design your doll.

DESIGN YOUR DOLL

The creation of a journal doll is not an exercise in realism. It is more about how you see yourself or the person you want to be than the nuts and bolts of your everyday life. Be prepared to change the way you view yourself as your doll takes form. This is a journey of self-discovery, and it's a journey worth taking.

+ Exaggerate your best features.

+ Increase the color saturation and intensity of your presence, from your eyes to your hair.

+ Design the body you want and cover yourself with the things you love that express your creative soul.

These three journal dolls by artist Kelli Perkins define three distinct roles of one woman: mother, artist, and librarian.

24"h × 7"w (61 × 18 cm)
Mixed-media art dolls with handpainted fabric and found objects

creating THE FACE

MATERIALS

Camera • Printer-ready fabric • Soft colored pencils • Sewing machine • Thread • Wool roving • Felting needle • Felting foam • Polyester fiberfill• Dyed or decorated muslin • Heavy interfacing • Permanent marker • Optional: Tyvek • Book pages • Beads • Buttons • Felt • Fibers • Ribbon • Angelina Fibers • Inks, iridescent paints • Block of wood • 12" Dowel • Heat gun• Fusible web • Pipe cleaners

1 Find a nice sunny spot and set up a tripod. Pull your hair back and take photos of yourself with different expressions. Look angelic, look surprised, look happy. If you wear glasses, take some with them on and some without. When you are satisfied that you have something to work with, upload the photos onto your computer and use image-editing software to alter them. Adjust the color and contrast so that your features are bold and the rest of your face is washed out.

2 Resize the images to about 3" long and print them on pre-treated inkjet-compatible fabric. Trim each face, leaving a small margin. Cut a 6" square of plain muslin and bond a face to the center with fusible web. Repeat with the remaining faces. Place a free-motion foot on your sewing machine and drop the feed dog. Using black thread, sew around the perimeter of each face, securing it to the muslin. Working slowly, follow the lines and contours of your face, outlining them with thread. Sew around your mouth, nose, eyes, and eyebrows, stitching and texturizing with the thread.

3 Color your face with soft artist's pencils. For the cheeks, lay the stitched face on top of a piece of felting foam. Pull a small tuft of wool roving to match the fabric you'll use for the base of your doll and wind it into a little ball. Punch it into the cheek area with a felting needle, picking up stray fibers as you go and incorporating them until you have a soft, round cheek. As you go along, occasionally pick the fabric up from the foam so that it doesn't become entangled.

4 Cut around the outside of the face, leaving a 1½" margin of muslin. Make the face into a little pillow by sewing a long gathering stitch all the way around the muslin. Pull the thread to loosely gather the fabric and stuff with fiberfill. Stitch closed on the back.

building A BASE

1 Create a doll template by drawing your chosen shape on a piece of card stock. Dolls come in a variety of shapes, so pick one that's pleasing to you. As a guideline, these dolls are about 15" long and 5" wide at the shoulder. Include an extra ¼" for the seam allowance.

2 Pin the template to the base fabric and cut two for each doll. Choose a fabric that represents your role. I spent some time dyeing fabric before I began. For one doll, I used beeswax resist to create x's and o's, then overstamped with gold paint. Another is dyed deep blue-green, stamped with text, and printed with a coffee cup stamp and acrylic paint. If you intend to journal on the back of your doll, don't make the color too dark or busy.

3 With right sides together, stitch around the edges of the body, leaving a ¼" seam allowance. Start at one side below the shoulder and stitch around the bottom, coming up to the base of the head on the other side. Leave the top of the head open. Turn right-side out and press lightly. Handsew the face pillow to the front of your doll.

1 To construct hair, cut a piece of heavy interfacing 1" × 3" to serve as a base. Choose stiff materials for the hair or add a stiffener like paper or interfacing so that it will stand up. Mix and match the following techniques to create a bundle of strips and then zigzag stitch them to the interfacing base.

- Glue bits of book text to strips of Tyvek. Spray with inks and iridescent paints. Roll around a pencil to curl.

- Bond strips of fabric to heavy interfacing with fusible web and cut into lengths.

- Wrap pipe cleaners with funky art fibers.

- Wind dyed cheesecloth or fabric around a pipe cleaner, then wrap with short lengths of Angelina fiber. Shrink the Angelina with short bursts from a heat gun.

- Braid funky fibers or strips of cloth.

- Cut pieces of wool or synthetic felt and stamp them. Sew a zigzag stitch down the center.

- Add silk or wool roving and ravels of fabric over the strips to fill out your doll's wig.

2 After you've made the strips and sewn them to the base piece, insert the interfacing base "hairpiece" into the top of the doll's head and topstitch around the head to close it, leaving a small hole in the side of the shoulder for stuffing. Finish stuffing your doll with fiberfill and whipstitch closed.

3 Determine whether you want found art, fabric, or fiber arms, or even wings! Here are some ideas:

- Bend a pipe cleaner in half, making a loop in the middle. Wrap it with fabric strips or fibers and attach a hand charm to the loop. Insert the other end inside the doll and stitch.

- Make two narrow tubes of fabric—turn and stuff for arms. To make the hands, cut two pieces of fabric and a piece of stiff interfacing in the shape of hands and topstitch together to form a sandwich. Sew the hand to the arm, then roll the other end under and attach it at the shoulders with hand stitching.

- Create hands by bending copper wire to form fingers. Wire hands to clothespins or other found objects and stitch to the sides of the doll. Tie on fibers.

4. To allow your doll to stand up, make a pocket in the back. Cut some matching 2" × 6" fabric strips and iron a ¼" seam allowance under on three sides. Handstitch an upside-down pocket to the back of the doll, lining the top edge of the pocket with the rise of the shoulders and leaving the bottom open. Embed a small 12" dowel rod into a block of wood and glue in place. Stain or paint the dowel. When it's dry, hang your journal doll on the dowel, using the pocket.

embellishing AND JOURNALING

1 Embellish your dolls in ways that are meaningful to you. For the mother doll, I stuffed and glued small hearts in my arms to represent my children, then beaded them. For my artist doll, I attached an old paintbrush and a ball of silk yarn. For my librarian doll, I added miniature books with quotations about reading. Use beads and scatter or even stack them. Sew on lots of luscious fibers, charms, and whimsical touches.

2 The final step is to turn your doll into a journal. On a notepad, journal your feelings about this role, using the words and symbols you've written down. Search for ways to describe how this role helps define you. When you are satisfied with the sentiments, take a fine permanent marker and transfer these thoughts to the back of the doll. You've created a meaningful representation of what you bring to the world and a permanent record of the thoughts that accompany your journey.

making **MINIATURE BOOKS**

MATERIALS

Fabric (such as painted muslin)
• Card stock • Watercolor paper
• Vintage buttons • Waxed linen
thread • Beads • Matte shrink
plastic • Alcohol inks • Fabric glue
• Ribbon • Text stamps • White
acrylic stamps • Nonstick mat

1 For each book, cut two 1½" × 3" pieces of fabric or painted muslin. Cut a piece of card stock to the same size. Sandwich the card stock between the fabric and sew around the edges, leaving a small seam allowance.

2 Cut two pieces of watercolor paper to 1½" × 3". Stack them on top of the fabric piece and stitch down the middle through all thicknesses to form a book.

3 Sew a vintage button to the cover. Stitch a 3" length of waxed linen thread to the back of the book, knot the ends, and attach a small bead. Wrap the thread around the button as a closure.

4 To make the book embellishments, cut some matte shrink plastic into 2" × 2" squares. Dye with alcohol inks, then stamp with a text stamp and white acrylic paint. Shrink according to instructions and flatten by covering with a nonstick mat and pressing. When cool, cut to fit the covers of your minibook. Attach with fabric glue.

5 Sew a ribbon along the spine and fill the book with thoughts about your doll and self.

> **"A single word even may be a spark of inextinguishable thought."**
>
> **—Percy Bysshe Shelley**

> "To furnish the means of acquiring knowledge is the greatest benefit that can be conferred upon mankind. It prolongs life itself and enlarges the sphere of existence."
>
> **—John Quincy Adams**

> "A book is a garden carried in the pocket."
>
> —Chinese proverb

MOTHER DOLL JOURNALING

"I am defined by the work of my hands as I care for the fruit of my soul. Healer, nurturer, protector, seamstress, songstress, bringer of harmony, keeper of promises. I wrap my blanket of peace around the ones I love. My hands cook meals to sustain life. My hands open up with unconditional love. My hands guide little hands through unfamiliar places to safety. Wherever I go I scatter petals of joy grown in the fields of my abundance. Whatever my family needs appears as if by magic."

LIBRARIAN DOLL JOURNALING

"I am defined by the work of my hands as I plow the unturned soil of collective wisdom, searching for sprouted truth. Reader, communicator, empowerer, investigator, infogoddess, puzzle solver, seeker, sage. I deliver answers to questions big and small. With my hands I open books and open worlds. With my hands I gather knowledge, satisfy curiosity, preserve understanding, honor culture, facilitate learning. With my hands I disperse a thousand years of history, one drop at a time."

ARTIST DOLL JOURNALING

"I am defined by the work of my hands as I shape the elements of the universe to my vision. Creator, diviner, builder, designer, gypsy dreamer. I give birth to color and scatter seeds of inspiration as I dance to the music of my muse. With my hands I mix media and layer juicy artfulness. With my hands I stitch and paint and draw and dye. I honor the funky, the eclectic, the bold, and bright. I take the wondrous beauty of nature and spill it upon my canvas."

capturing a LIFE IN PROGRESS

Rembrandt made some ninety self-portraits over the course of his lifetime, in part to keep a record of himself through the years. Each one reveals something about himself, his work, and his times. Making a life-in-progress self-portrait is a great way to take a snapshot of where you are: check in with yourself, take inventory, celebrate the accomplishments, realize the growth from challenges, count your blessings, be present, and look to the future. It's a great way to focus on the moment, and then, when the moment has passed, be able to look back and remember.

where have i been? WHERE AM I GOING?

By Kelly Rae Roberts

We are all collections of thoughts. Of memories. Of moments in our lives that stand still and moments that speak out loud. To me, self-portraits are a way to honor these moments in our lives. Like a journal that captures who we are as our life unfolds, self-portraits allow us to explore ourselves, get to know ourselves a bit more, and reveal our inner story and truth.

In my midtwenties (before I had joined the self-portrait revolution), I found myself in a vague and confusing place of having lost sight of who I was. For years, I had gone with the grain, always agreeable, always easy-going, always saying yes. Married . . . check. House . . . check. Job . . . check. Vacation time . . . check. Garden . . .

check. Passion and inspiration . . . not so much. Although I had a loving husband whom I adored and who was always encouraging me to find my passion, I began to feel unfamiliar toward myself and a bit misdirected. I wondered: Where did I go? What were my likes? Dislikes? Who was I, really?

As a way to rediscover and unearth my real self (underneath the layers of yeses), I started taking photos. Over time, I found that by taking photos of not just myself, but of the things I love, I began to remind myself who I was. It turns out that I was a girl who liked to wear red shoes, yellow shoes, and even turquoise shoes! I noticed (and loved) heart shapes everywhere—in the trees, in the clouds, in flattened gum on the sidewalk. I was a girl who looked up to see the sky. Whose grin wanted to be captured on film. Whose everyday simplicities brought growth and abundance. Self-portraiture, simply taking photos of myself and of the things in my daily life that resonated with me, reawakened me to myself. It was a joyous rediscovery, and I will always be grateful for it.

Self-portraits, whether they're a photo of myself or something that represents who I am, continue to allow me to capture my life in progress as I grow and change and reach and dream. It gives me the opportunity to really know myself in the present moment, to attach meaning to who I am so that I don't wake up one day, like I did so many years ago, and realize that I had forgotten who I was.

For me, each painting I create is a self-portrait of its own, a signature of a single step in my journey. As the paintings continue and change, so do I. My tastes in color changes. My tones. My hairstyles. My wishes. My dreams. Everything I create is a reflection of myself. Like everything in life, it's all connected.

For this painting, titled *this is me*, I wanted to show some bits and pieces of who I am today. Intermingled throughout the painting are photographs of the things I most treasure: me at my favorite places (the Oregon coast) and with my favorite people (my husband and my momma). If you look closely, you will find images of my meaningful things, like my yellow shoes, letters from family and friends, my beloved dog Bella, my favorite tree, my green bike, a heart-shaped rock, sea glass, my favorite white chair in my studio space. These are all things that make me who I am today, in this space, in this life. I wanted to capture it in a painting that would tell the story of my life today.

Here I am. Take a walk with me. This is me. This is my self-portrait painting.

In this collaged and painted self-portrait, Kelly Rae builds layers of her life and paints on them, only to wipe the paint away to expose the really wonderful and meaningful aspects.

9"w × 12"h × 2"d (23 × 31 × 5 cm)
Mixed-media collage with paint

painting YOUR LIFE

1 Gather your favorite photos and, if you have not already, upload them to your computer. Choose photos that speak about who you are: family, work space, favorite treasures. Alter or edit as desired and print on heavy matte paper using an ink-jet printer.

2 Crop and trim the photographs and randomly glue them onto a 9" × 12" canvas using gel medium (I like to use Golden gel medium in gloss). Once the entire canvas is covered with your patchwork of photographs, coat the entire canvas with gel medium. Once dry, use a charcoal pencil to sketch a simple outline of the girl over the collage.

3 Mix a small amount of fluid acrylic paints to get a soft green. Roll a brayer through the paint until saturated with color, then roll the brayer over the collaged background. Be careful to stay outside the lines of the sketched figure. Then, while the paint is still wet, wipe away sections of the paint with a dampened paper towel to reveal the images underneath. Repeat this entire step with a light yellow acrylic paint after the green paint has dried.

4 Using a paintbrush, fill in the girl's dress with pink fluid acrylic paint on the top and brown on the bottom. Again, while the paint is still wet, use a dampened cloth to wipe away sections of the paint to reveal the photos underneath. Repeat this step until you achieve your desired effect of the dress looking like a small patchwork of personal imagery.

5 Fill in her face, hair, and legs with ink (I like to use the Ranger Adirondack ink pads) and charcoal pencil. I wanted to use ink on her face, rather than paint, so that the words of the letter (written to me by my beloved sister) would show through her skin.

6 Paint the wings with white fluid acrylics. Paint the entire bottom half of the painting with the same soft green used earlier in the painting. To me, this made the painting less busy and it grounded the figure a bit more.

Of course, by painting the bottom half of the painting, several of the photos I had collaged in the beginning stages were now covered up. To me, this carries meaning. Perhaps these images were serendipitously thrown in for process's sake alone, just for me to see, to remember. Just as in life, some images are more prominent in our hearts, and some are in the background, covered up by layers of paint, experience, and feeling. This is okay. It's the painting and the process that are all about self-discovery, even if it means some beloved images are ultimately painted over. In paintings like this one that carry such personal meaning, bits and pieces of me are there all along, in the forefront, in the background, in the memory of all the images, covered or not.

I finished the painting by adding the words "this is me" on her chest.

MATERIALS

- Favorite photos uploaded onto the computer • Heavy matte paper • Ink-jet printer • Gel medium • Charcoal pencil • Fluid acrylic paints in green, yellow, white, pink • Brayer • Palette paper • Dampened paper towel, cloth • Paintbrush • Ink pad

This overpainted patchwork of memories is exposed by wiping paint away before it dries. Look closely to see the layers of materials.

quotes for loving life

Kelly Rae Roberts loves these quotes and hopes you can use them for inspiration in your art and your life.

"The aim of life is to live, and to live means to be aware; joyously, drunkenly, serenely, divinely aware."
—Henry Miller

"Feel yourself being quietly drawn by the deeper pull of what you truly love."
—Rumi

"There are years that ask questions and years that answer."
—Zora Neale Hurston

"We do not remember days, we remember moments"
—Cesare Pavese

"I don't want to get to the end of my life and find that I lived just the length of it. I want to have lived the width of it as well."
—Diane Ackerman

"The journey between what you once were and who you are now becoming is where the dance of life really takes place."
—Barbara De Angelis

"If I were called upon to state in a few words the essence of everything I was trying to say, it would be something like this: Listen to your life. See it for the fathomless mystery that it is. In the boredom and pain of it no less than in the excitement and gladness: Touch, taste, smell your way to the holy and hidden heart of it because in the last analysis, all moments are key moments, and life itself is grace."
—Frederick Buechner

"When nothing is sure, Everything is possible"
—Marge Drabble

"Freedom is what you do with what's been done to you."
—Jean-Paul Sartre

"Ahh, yes. This IS me. A painting, a self-portrait, a life . . . me."
—Kelly

Lighter-colored paints and inks will allow more delicate images and text to show through.

documenting A YEAR

The times we live in shape us. Politics, music, technology, literature, fashion, mores—they all have an effect on us and our choices in life, to some degree. Using the year you were born as inspiration for a self-portrait automatically gives you images and symbols to work with, even though you can't actually remember what happened. Another way to approach this concept is to look back on a more recent significant year or keep an art journal in real time. You could make quilt pages or squares every week or month or commit to one tiny piece of art a day—small collaged chipboard or fabric squares or baseball-card-size works, like artist trading cards. At the end of the year, put them together as a book or illustrations for a journal, as a quilt, or as a mosaic. Remember, you don't have to include a physical likeness of yourself: a paper napkin from the restaurant where your beloved proposed, a rock from the beach to which you retreated after finishing your doctorate, a shiny penny from the year you were born—it all adds up to you.

1967: MY YEAR, MYSELF
(an alternative self-portrait) By Debbi Crane

If you were ever to catch me singing to myself, I would probably be singing a Janis Joplin song. Not because I grew up listening to her or because I remember when her songs were first on the radio, but because the truth in her voice is so compelling. I was born in the spring before 1967's Summer of Love, just as "The Pearl," with Big Brother and the Holding Company, was beginning her short and tortured rise to fame. Since I can remember, I have had a fascination with Janis, Sgt. Pepper's, hippies, and all things '67, even though I have no actual memories of that storied year.

In 2007, I celebrated my fortieth birthday. With this milestone, I set out to make a book about the best year ever, my year, 1967. This is arguably the most important year of my life—you don't have anything without a beginning. But the challenge was this: How could I make a book about a year, however culturally influential, that I don't even remember? I began with the large and messy mental catalog of 1967 trivia I have gathered over the years. Inside, I dug up some gems, such as the first Super Bowl, the tragic death of Gus Grissom, and the release of Jacqueline Susann's novel, *Valley of the Dolls*. Internet research helped me discover that Aretha Franklin recorded and released "Respect" in 1967, that John and Yoko started spending a lot of time together, and that a Beach Boy was arrested for draft evasion. As I studied, I made long lists, scribbled notes and doodles in my sketchbook, and imagined the many forms this book could take.

As I began to make the actual book, I discovered that seven rectangles folded in half and nested together made the exact number of pages for a front cover, a back cover, and twenty-six pages. This is a magic number in book arts; there are twenty-six letters in the alphabet, so this would make the perfect abecedarium, or alphabet book, with no extra pages. Making an abecedarium is a great way to create focus and organization with disparate bits of information and imagery.

I began to choose entries for the letters by listing the alphabet in my sketchbook. For some letters, I instantly came up with multiple possibilities; for other letters, like K and Q, I struggled to find just the right word. I gave myself very loose guidelines: the letter of the alphabet didn't have to be the first letter in the word; for example, I could use Bob Dylan for Y and Peter Max for X. The book was, after all, for me, so I could make up my own rules as I went along.

For the actual book structure, I adopted a "flea-bitten fabulous" aesthetic; I wanted it to look as dirty as the bottom of a hippie's bare feet yet as colorful as her embroidered dashiki. The covers and pages are made of raw-edged canvas duck coated with acrylic paint and unevenly

stained with walnut ink. Canvas is sturdier than paper, but just as easy to fold, sew, and embellish. For the cover, I stitched on a piece of tie-dyed muslin and a hint of flower power.

As a finished book, I think *1967: My Year, Myself* fulfills three important requirements I have for my work. It is inviting to viewers, with the variety of colors and tactile feel of the fabric pages. The content is interesting to read, both the historical facts and the commentary. I hope, above all, that this book inspires others to look back at influential times in their lives and create commemorative artwork with strong personal significance.

Tiny tabs on this book allude to significant themes and topics in Debbi's birth-year book.

6½" square closed, 13"w × 6½"h open
Fabric book with mixed media

Even before I had decided on how I would represent each letter of the alphabet, I began to work on the pages. When I'm making a book, I get excited about creating the content and run ahead of myself, even if I'm not sure where I'm going. For the letters for which I had already figured out the word, I drew doodley images on plain white paper and colored them with watercolor and colored pencil. I made the drawings as I had time and ideas, not all in one sitting. I worked on the pages before the book was bound, giving me access to several pages at once. I used acrylic paint for the letter on each page, varying the placement depending on what else would be on that page. The pages are edged with Caran d'Ache watercolor crayons, which I painted over with water and worked into the raw edges of the pages.

After allowing the paint and watercolor crayons to dry, I used permanent markers in various widths and colors to write the majority of the text in my own handwriting. (I hope we are all over hating our handwriting by now. Nothing makes a book feel more personal than actual handwriting.) Some pages contain only words; others contain imagery as well. All the pictures in the book are my drawings, but photocopied images or clip art could be used instead. I chose to make drawings that were sketchy and symbolic, not faithful renderings of the subjects. The drawings were glued to the pages with sparingly applied white craft glue.

To integrate the image and text, I applied more watercolor crayons around and in between. With the majority of the pages complete, it was time to bind the book together. I chose a simple binding that required only three sewing stations. This binding also allowed me to carry the 1967 theme through to the spine with the use of jute twine and beads.

I'm never happy with a flat, square-edged book. You can buy a plain, flat book. Why bother to make one? I like to add little teases to the edges of some pages to generate curiosity. In "1967," I used eyelets to attach small watercolored tags to a few pages. I also added some three-dimensional elements to some of the pages in the form of silk flowers, pom-poms, and pearls. As a final touch, I created bits of editorial text on the computer. I colored and outlined them with pencil, cut them out, and glued them to the pages. This text consisted of my thoughts and comments on the people and events in the book.

The U.S. and the U.S.S.R. signed a nuclear nonproliferation treaty

I guess it worked out okay.

I don't think a country that doesn't even

exist anymore can blow us up.

NO NUKES

sock it to m

The book came out in 67 and growing up, but never got it when I understood what a big deal it was when it came out R.I.P. Sharon Tate.

I saw the film many times

the movie followed in 68

Valley the Dolls

Unfortunately, Squeaky met Charlie in February, 1967.

making your own BIRTH-YEAR BOOK

1 Coat both sides of the duck with the white acrylic. Allow to dry between coats and before flipping over to paint the other sides. Don't worry about neatness. I like to use two to three coats of paint on each side.

2 Stain the dry canvas with walnut ink. Allow the ink to puddle in places. Let the ink dry overnight, then flip the canvases over and stain the other sides.

3 Sew the 5" × 11" pieces of fabric to one of the canvas pieces for the cover. Either machine stitch or handsew into place.

4 Fold all seven canvas pieces in half and nest together, with the cover on the outside.

5 Open the book flat over an old book or a thick stack of scrap cardboard. Use your awl to pierce through all of the pages on the spine crease at the center, about ¾" from the top edge and about ¾" from the bottom edge.

6 Thread the embroidery needle with the waxed linen thread and tie a knot in the end.

7 Begin sewing inside the book. Sew out through the top sewing station. Lay the four cords of twine alongside the spine. Sew over the cords and back into the top station.

8 Sew out through the center station, over the cords, and back into the center station.

9 Repeat for the last station. Tie a knot in the waxed thread inside the spine and trim end.

10 Add beads or charms to the ends of the jute.

MATERIALS

7 pieces of white or natural canvas duck, 6" × 12" • I piece of lightweight fabric for the cover, 5" × 11" • White acrylic paint • Walnut ink • Collage materials of your choice • Colorants of your choice: paints, watercolor crayons, colored pencils, and permanent markers • 4 pieces jute twine (or similar material depending on the theme of your book), each 12"–18" • waxed linen book-binding thread, 18" • Awl • Embroidery needle • Paintbrush • Sewing machine or needle and thread • Beads or charms, if desired

Summer of Love

This is the ONLY episode of Star Trek I have ever seen. It was in the unit on reproduction, I think. It was in health. Premiered in 1967. I saw it in seventh grade

The Trouble with Tribbles

Your birth-year book can be filled with any type of imagery you wish. Here Debbi has used her own sketches, but images from print media and advertisements or just words would work as well.

more *year-worthy topics*

This concept can be adapted to other significant years in your life. You can focus on the culture of the times or include "scenes" from your own life during that year. Here are some other special-year topics you might tackle:

+ My fiftieth birthday (or other significant birthday)
+ My first year as a new mom (or baby's first year)
+ The first year of our marriage
+ My graduation year
+ My year of quitting [insert vice here]
+ Our first year in our new home
+ My first year postdivorce
+ My first year as a full-time artist

"I hope, above all, that this book inspires others to look back at influential times in their lives and create commemorative artwork with strong personal significance."

—Debbi

self-portrait MASKS

The mask form is a paradox: It conforms to our shape and yet hides our expression. A mask can conceal our public self and allow us the freedom to reveal our true self. It can help us face our fears (by putting on a facade of courage when we're trembling inside) or hide from them (by taking on a different identity). Wearing a mask is powerful and intimate. The experience ultimately reveals not just the face you present to the world, but the one you present to your self. The truth is, we wear many "masks." Each one divulges or hides a different part of our selves. The mask—or masks—you make as art can do the same.

pieces OF ME
By Chrysti Hydeck

Self-portraits intimidate me. In fact, they make me extremely uncomfortable. I don't particularly like creating them. I don't particularly like looking at them. I don't particularly like sharing them.

Yes, I said it: I don't like self-portraits. Well, that is, I don't like my own self-portraits.

Now that may seem odd, considering I am contributing to this book—but please, allow me to explain. I don't have to like something to find it fascinating or beneficial.

I have never found that internal peace where one fully comes to terms with who they are, who they really are. A complete acceptance of one's self, if you will. Frankly, I'm not sure if I ever want to. I have some deeply rooted fear that if I accept myself in the entirety, I will stop finding reasons to grow, and learn . . . and, well . . . live.

It is not that I don't like myself. I do. It is just that I see myself in pieces. I look at life in pieces. I create in pieces. The "big picture," in any aspect of my life, is both overwhelming and disturbing to me. I'm not comfortable with who I am physically or even emotionally as a whole, but within those small pieces of me I am content. So, I focus on the details. It is, after all, the sum of all those pieces, all those parts, that creates the whole me.

Part of my joy in making art is the fantasy and illusion it contains. Within my creations, I can alter reality and push the boundaries imposed on the world. Self-portraits defy that, since I used to see them as painfully real. But once I began seeing these captivating, amazing self-portrait photographs and mixed-media pieces online, they intrigued me, and I secretly yearned to try some of my own.

What you find on these pages is just a few of several masks I have created to date. Each mask is distinctly different; they evolve as I do. Each mask is an accurate reflection of some part of my personality or appearance. Not all are pretty, because I am not always pretty. In fact, some blatantly show my dark side. Each mask is a part of who I am, who I was, and who I want to become. Most important, each and every mask is not just composed of elements that represent me, but has become a piece of me itself.

Creating these masks has given me an outlet to heal, presented me with new challenges, and altered how I see myself. It is a process that has allowed me to begin saying: I like self-portraits. I like my own self-portraits.

With this particular mask, Chrysti chose to use a torn paper background, as it helps the structural integrity of the mask and fit the "pieces of me" theme. It's up to you to decide what you want your own mask to reflect. Try to think out a plan before starting; whether it's a color scheme or a symbolic theme you have in mind.

12"w × 12"h (31 × 31 cm)
Plaster, mixed-media collage, and assemblage

making THE MASK

MATERIALS

Plaster cloth • Petroleum jelly • Plastic wrap • Scissors • Shallow pan or bowl of warm water • Mirror • Paper towels

1 Gather your supplies and sit down in front of a mirror. Cut plaster cloth into a variety of different-size strips—6" × 2" (15 × 5 cm), 3" × ½" (8 × 1 cm), 4" × 2" (10 × 5 cm)—and a few narrow, short pieces for the nose. Keep scissors handy while applying the cloth to your face so you can cut and shape the pieces as needed.

2 To prevent the plaster cloth from sticking to your hair and skin, wrap plastic wrap over your hairline and allow it to overlap onto your face a bit while trying to keep it as smooth as possible. Generously apply petroleum jelly over your entire face, neck, and ears. Be sure to apply it inside your nostrils and to put an extra-thick coating on any areas with hair, such as the hairline, eyebrows, and eyelashes.

3 Now you will begin to apply the plaster—work as quickly as possible to ensure the smoothest possible surface for your mask. Dip a long strip of the plaster cloth into the water. Holding it above the pan, use your fingers to smooth out the cloth and remove any excess moisture.

4 Place the strip horizontally over the middle of your nose, pressing it into the contours of your face while allowing it to extend to both cheeks. Be sure to smooth the plaster cloth with your fingers as you apply it.

5 Apply another piece in the same manner, overlapping the first piece as you apply it to your skin. You want this piece to extend to the edges of your face, on each side. Pay special attention to where the pieces meet and smooth the seam as much as possible with your fingers.

6 Continue dipping and placing the pieces on your face; overlapping each piece with the ones placed prior. Work the edges of your mask first (chin, hairline, forehead, and neck if desired), then fill in the gaps. Along the edge of your mask, place the long pieces vertically. Smooth each piece as with the first.

7 Continue the process until the mask is four to five layers thick. The nostril area only requires two to three layers; after all, you do want to breathe!

    OPTIONAL: For the smoothest possible finish, use full-width pieces of the plaster cloth over your entire face as the final layer. This is not so important if you are going to be texturizing the finished surface, collaging, or otherwise embellishing.

8 Allow the mask to set while on your face, about fifteen to twenty minutes. You'll start to feel the change as it loosens and becomes a bit warm to the touch while hardening. To help pass the time, go scare the neighbors or snap a few photos of yourself; these make great self-portraits to use in other projects.

9 Wriggle your eyebrows, crinkle your nose, and let your lips squirm gently to help free the mask from your skin. Remove the mask by slowly rocking the edges loose from your face. To avoid undue stress on the edges, gently rock the mask in a down-and-away motion.

10 Let the mask air-dry for twenty-four hours. Impatient? Place it in the oven, on a foil-covered pan at 200°F for fifteen to twenty minutes.

more mask tips

Follow Chrysti's advice for a no-fail mask:

✦ **TO DO THE NOSE:** Use the tiny pieces and work them just slightly into your nostrils.

✦ **TO DO THE EYES:** If you are self-applying the cloths, you should leave the eyes uncovered. Cut a few triangle-shaped pieces of the plaster cloth to better work into the shape of your eyes, and cover as much of the area as possible while still being able to see.

✦ **TO DO THE LIPS:** Do your mouth last and only apply three layers to help retain some detail and shape.

"We're always attracted to the edges of what we are, out by the edges where it's a little raw and nervy."
—E. L. Doctorow

For this mixed-media on canvas mask, artist Chrysti Hydeck shows the solace she finds inside a monochromatic palette when her life feels chaotic. "The mask process is what I find most soothing . . . it's calming, messy, carefree, gratifying, and so easy to lose myself in," she says.

12"w × 12"h (31 × 31 cm)
Mixed media on canvas including plaster cast of hand and face, dried flowers, vintage doorbell, paint, wood bark, ephemera, doodles, vintage measuring tape, clothespin, feathers, seashells, and more

personalizing your mask

Your mask can be as personal or as impersonal as you'd like. Use the following ideas to help jump-start your own creative process:

+ Use feathers for eyebrows or eyelashes.

+ Use permanent markers to doodle, "tattoo," or otherwise draw on your mask.

+ Apply sequins, glitter, or microbeads to the lips or around the eyes to highlight them.

+ Use gel medium to adhere other collage elements, text, or additional papers.

+ Use bundles of dried flowers in the eyes.

+ Drill holes in the sides, use lush ribbons and fibers or elastic to make it a wearable mask.

+ Shred old letters, diary pages, or personal ephemera and curl with scissors for hair.

+ Use chalks to act as blusher and seal with a fixative.

+ Use tear-shaped gems as teardrops under the eyes.

+ Put old photographs behind the eye openings, allowing them to act as frames.

+ Use giant faux flowers over the eyes.

+ Write a secret message on the lips, stamp on a favorite quote.

+ Paint on features or patterns.

+ Glue a button over the center of the lip.

+ Glue piping or fibers along the edge of the mask.

+ Make a fabric ruffle to go under the neck.

+ Thread wire with beads and curl into funky and fun shapes for hair.

+ Cover the entire mask in moss and add butterfly and flower embellishments.

+ Attach the mask to a stick or pole and place it inside a vase for an unusual bloom.

---

sealing THE MASK

1 Lightly sand any bumpy or rough areas of the mask. A nail file helps tremendously when doing the eye and nostril areas.

2 Beginning with the inside of the mask, brush on a thin, light coat of gel medium and allow it to dry. Repeat six to eight times or until hard. Check the mask in between coats to see if any of the plaster cloth is turning up; if it has, use gel medium to adhere it back in place. Allow it to dry completely.

3 Flip your mask over, and repeat the same process as above. Resist the desire to put on thick coats and to save time by coating both sides at once. It is crucial to apply thin coats of the gel medium and not allow it to make the mask "wet." Otherwise, the mask will start to lose its shape, and possibly fall apart.

4 Sand or file any clumpy areas around the nostrils and eyes where gel medium may have accumulated.

TIP: You know you have applied enough layers of gel medium when the mask isn't as flexible or fragile to the touch.

MATERIALS

Sandpaper • Nail file • Gel medium • Paintbrushes

collaging THE FACE

1   Pick papers that hold meaning or value to you—copies of photographs, ephemera, bits of decorative papers from projects you have done. Tear them into various-size pieces, ink the edges if desired, and place them near you for easy accessibility.

2   Brush a generous coat of gel medium across a portion of your mask.

3   While the gel medium is still wet, arrange and firmly press your torn papers onto the mask, smoothing with your fingers as you go. (Remember to wipe off your fingers with baby wipes so the clumps that dry don't get onto the mask.) Apply more gel medium as needed and brush another thin coat on top of the papers. Continue this process until the entire mask is covered. Allow to cure overnight. In the nostril and eye areas, work the papers over the rim and onto the back side for a flawless finish.

4   Brush the acrylic glaze over the entire mask. Use paper towels and baby wipes to remove the glaze in spots you want to highlight. Allow to dry. Repeat if desired.

5   Using a foam brush, spread the antiquing gel over the entire surface. Use a heavier application in the spots where you see dents and crevices. Allow it to sit for a few minutes, and then use a paper towel to wipe it off. If you'd like more of it removed, use a baby wipe. Reapply in specific spots if desired.

MATERIALS

Torn papers • Acrylic glaze (or gel medium tinted with paint) • Antiquing gel • Paintbrushes • Foam brush • Paper towels • Baby wipes • Gel medium

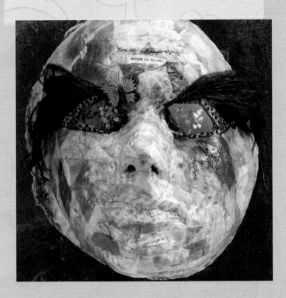

mask making as a healing tool

I've grown up knowing I was different. I moved differently, I thought differently, I acted differently. For me, it's always just simply been a part of who I am; but for most other people the fact that I live with Tourette syndrome and bipolar disorder, is often misunderstood. How I am judged, treated, and perceived is frequently affected by this viewpoint. I have never quite felt that I truly belonged anywhere—until I began focusing on creating as my career.

Suddenly, all that set me apart, made me stand out in a way that people could relate to. After all, these disorders I was born with have facets that anyone can identify with. My enthusiasm and belief that anyone can and should create gave me a way to connect with people on a level I had never experienced.

Mask making takes creating to its rawest form. You work on the most challenging canvas: a rough version of your own physical shape. It allows you to visualize who you are, where you have been, and what you'd like to become. It's a wondrous experience that you can't escape from. Starting with that very first strip you place on you face, until the last embellishment has been added and you feel yourself transform. You see your issues work themselves out, and you notice all the amazing qualities within you that are often overlooked day to day. It heals, it soothes, and it immerses you in a way that no other form allows. Don't just take my word for it—to understand its true power you need to try it for yourself.

creating THE CANVAS BACKGROUND

MATERIALS

Canvas board • Modeling paste • Acrylic paint (three to four shades of one primary color) • Old credit card • Heat gun • Antiquing gel, stain, or brown ink

1 Tint the modeling paste with paint, and use the credit card to apply a thick layer to your canvas. You want this to be extra thick in some areas, anywhere from ½" (1 cm) to ¾" (2 cm), so that it will crack as it shrinks. Let the credit card edges add additional texture as well.

2 Use a heat gun to apply heat over the modeling paste. Drying it quickly is the key to getting it to shrink and crack in spots. You'll see it start to dry, crack, and shrink as you apply the heat.

3 Because we put on such a thick application, it will need to air-dry (at least overnight) to make sure the underlying paste is dry as well. If you try to play with it too soon (despite the exterior seeming dry), you risk ruining your work, as it will glob up and scrape right off.

4 Once it is dry, start painting, blending as desired. Mix in a tiny touch of gray paint to add a shadowy feel in spots.

5 Use the heat gun to apply heat to the wet paint. For additional texture, hold it still in some spots until you see a few bubbles appear; quickly move it from that area once you see them and go to another section of your painting. After it is dry, you can choose to add more layers of paint and paste if desired.

6 Just as we did on the mask, brush the antiquing gel over the entire surface. Let it pool up in the cracks and crevices. Allow it to sit for a few minutes, then use a paper towel to wipe it off. If you'd like more of it removed, use a baby wipe instead. Reapply in particular spots if desired.

masks throughout history

Masks are filled with symbolism that you can use to guide your own creation.

AFRICAN TRIBAL MASKS If you were an animal, who would you be? Throughout history, humans have identified with animals and used animal masks to explore and identify their nature. African tribes often wear animal masks at ceremonies; for example, the antelope mask represents the hardworking farmer.

SHAMAN MASK Shamans the world over have used masks in their sacred ceremonies. They often resemble animals or have tassels of feathers and other natural objects attached. Your shamanic self-portrait mask can be therapeutic, with symbols, imagery, embellishments, and colors to help you heal.

MASQUERADE MASKS Used for carnival celebrations as well as fancy-dress balls, these colorful masks usually have dramatic, fanciful shapes and rich colors and textures. This style can be used to celebrate yourself or reveal your inner eighteenth-century countess.

WAR MASKS The ancient Greeks and the Chinese were famous for wearing grotesque masks on their heads or shields during battle, hoping to frighten the enemy. Your war mask can express anger or help you "do battle" with something frightening in yourself or your life.

attaching the MASK TO THE BACKGROUND

When incorporating your mask into the canvas, you have a plethora of options. Some of my favorites are:

✦ Using strips of plaster cloth to connect the mask to the canvas board, making it one with the canvas. Then paint and finish as desired.

✦ Incorporating casts of your hands with your face for a moving piece.

✦ Attaching a hook to your canvas and hanging the mask on the hook, a great way to make it a removable piece.

✦ Using a hinge to make the mask like a door.

✦ Drilling through the canvas and mask and using ribbons, fabric strips, rope, or fibers to thread through it.

This mask is attached to the canvas background with a hinge so that it can swing open.

using *objects* TO TELL A STORY

Objects can be touchstones to our true selves. The choice of objects, their shape and texture, their symbolism and juxtaposition—all can help you tell a story through your artwork. A story about you. The objects you begin with can be found items that have significance to or about you. Or you can select them for their physical properties (a curved piece of metal to represent a smile or glitter to connote glamour).

When creating a self-portrait through assemblage, think of the objects as an outline—the main points of the story. Add elements such as paint, patina, and fabric (the rough draft) and then refine it with text, trim, and other embellishments. Pay attention as you make your choices: The items you choose to include and those you decide to reject will tell you something about yourself as a person and also what you're learning as an artist.

Everything in this assemblage bares a piece of Jenn Mason's soul. For example, the whitewashing is representative of clean slates as the artist "would rather open a new checkbook than balance her existing one," she says.

14"w × 9"h × 3"d (36 × 23 × 8 cm)
Mixed-media assemblage with found objects

mixed-media ASSEMBLAGE

By Jenn Mason

No matter what piece of art I'm working on, I suppose that at least a little of it is actually a self-portrait of sorts. Most of my art revolves around telling stories—many times with actual words. As each collage or assemblage starts out, it begins to tell me its own narrative. Sometimes the story is coherent from start to finish. Sometimes the story transforms like the *Choose Your Own Adventure* books I used to read as a child. One thought, picture, found element, or word segues into the next. Many of the bits only make sense to me—some are secrets, some are inside jokes, some are painful realizations that I only understand once I've put them on canvas.

The challenge of creating this self-portrait was exhilarating. When I was working on this piece, I was also making paper jewelry for another book, designing packaging and samples for a new product, executing final edits on my most recent manuscript, and moving into my newly renovated carriage house. To put it simply, I was juggling. In the back of my mind the thought of this self-portrait kept percolating. Every day I'd pull something out of my closet to consider, contemplate, and reevaluate for the self-portrait. I also thought about what I wanted to say about myself. How exposed did I want to feel?

In the end, I decided that I wanted to represent myself like the Dutch masters who painted still lifes where everything in the painting had a specific meaning. In my case, though, I'd use a three-dimensional approach. I put my thoughts in a sieve and let all the petty or superficial things fall away. It didn't matter that I did or didn't lose ten pounds, or that my hair is short, and that I like chocolate (really, how many people don't?). Instead, I focused on what floated to the top; you know, the cream!

It seems a little odd to fully explain my art in detail, but the process has really been fulfilling and a little eye-opening. I highly recommend trying to approach creating a self-portrait in as many different ways as possible. I know I'm not going to stop with this one. I will also continue to tell my story through my other artwork—with a little piece of me in each one.

"The little oil can shown (left) is fittingly labeled 'self-doubt remover' because the self-portrait needs to represent the truth—and the truth is that I have an overactive self-doubt gland," artist Jenn Mason says. "This is something I continue to work on daily."

Jenn's soul

If you look into my eyes—really look—you can see my hopes and dreams (because I've put the words behind the camera lenses).

Different compartments signify a complex personality.

Bright green is my signature color, also representing my need for new beginnings.

Flowers are a treasure to the soul.

The entire box is whitewashed to represent the need to start with a clean slate.

A keyhole at first glance implies that I am closed off but upon further inspection says "soul within." Turn the key and come inside.

The heart and found text, "one I love," represent my husband, one of my favorite things.

A half-full glass represents undying optimism and is also filled with my tools of the trade.

A house with love on the door represents my family.

The support brace with two tacks symbolizes my daughters, who hold me together with their need for a strong mother.

The number 21. Why? Not sure; perhaps because that is how old I feel every day.

The wheels are the feet that keep me going—I am never still.

construction **TIPS**

To seal wood like the box used for the base of this piece, paint the whole piece with GAC 100 by Golden Paints first. (I use Golden Acrylic Paints, fluid acrylics, gel mediums, glazes, and extenders on my art because I can safely mix them together without worrying about how they'll interact.)

When attaching pieces together, try any of the following techniques:

1 Wire one of the legs through a drilled hole and secure the wire around the "21" screen tack.

2 Use soft gel medium as glue for bulky items.

3 Drill holes in the camera face with a hand-crank drill and hammer small finishing nails through the holes to secure.

4 Wrap thicker-gauge wire around the doll arms and then insert into a predrilled hole, making a small spiral inside the box to keep the wire from coming out.

5 Carpet tacks are wonderful for a variety of attachments.

6 You can create decorative tops for screws by gluing embellishments to the tops of them with gel medium. On this piece, metal flowers were glued to the tops of screws that were randomly screwed into one of the small compartments.

Jenn's number one tip for creating an assemblage such as this is to collect! "I walk a service dog for a friend, and I always find little doodads on my walks that I can use in my art," she says. "I also love flea markets and garage sales. Think beyond the item you see and think about what you could do with it if you took it apart. You never know what you might discover."

documenting yourself IN PHOTOS

One of the hardest images for an artist to create is a photographic self-portrait. The intimidation factor that lies beneath the project can be subtle and fierce—it is one thing to create an abstract likeness of oneself through patterns, textures, colors, and objects, but a whole different story when you have to look a camera lens dead in the eye. But, you see, that is where the beauty and freedom lies, for there is no rule that says your photographic self-portrait must be a straight-up face shot. It can be angled to disguise your face or show your best features. It can be zoomed in or zoomed out as much as you wish. And if you have a digital camera, you can experiment as much as you like without wasting a single art supply. If you get into the regular habit of snapping self-portraits, you'll have a visual growth chart that will speak volumes about you. Use the camera to tell all of your stories, document your roles, celebrate your wrinkles, entertain your ego, and, ultimately, capture the you that you wish others could see.

WHICH JANE to depict

By Jane LaFazio

The very first decision to be made in this assignment was how to interpret "self-portrait." Should I meditate and try to determine what color my aura is? Should I journal and determine my true personality and illustrate that? I have been collecting my broken drugstore reading glasses for years now, planning to do a portrait using them, since I'm totally dependent on them! Finally, I decided to use a realistic image as a starting point, but which one? My high school yearbook photo, or a recent snapshot or something in between on the timeline of photos of me? And then it hit me. I spotted those strips of black-and-white photos from the photo booth at the fair on my bulletin board. I knew I had my starting place and format.

When I was a kid, my girlfriends and I would spend fifty cents and get strips of photobooth portraits downtown or at the mall. For each photo, we'd make a goofy face, or change our hair or hat or glasses, become movie stars or punks within those moments as the camera clicked automatically. Four chances to try out a new persona! We waited the interminable three minutes for the photos to be magically developed, and then we'd giggle and scream at the hysterical images. Those black-and-white photo strips would be tucked in our bedroom mirror frames or on the bulletin board above our desk for a few weeks until they were replaced by more silly photos. Gosh, I wish I had those childhood mementos now.

The childhood tradition continues when my husband and I attend the annual county fair. We make sure to stop by the photobooth for a set of goofy photos, continuing the tradition of a new and sillier pose at each click of the camera. I've saved the photos over the last fifteen years or so, and they are wonderful to look back on. The fact that they are so consistent in appearance and routine, after all these years, makes them somehow an authentic record of our times.

Since this was a self-portrait assignment, I couldn't include my husband in the quilt. It will be fun to make one of him and me the next time!

As I study the finished piece, I see that I did a realistic portrait, in terms of size, proportion, and color in a flat, simplistic way. I could have stitched or drawn in the wrinkles and detail that makes a fifty-seven-year-old face, I suppose, but why? I see that face every day!

It was interesting and slightly challenging doing a portrait of myself from different angles, with different facial expressions. It would be fun to do a similar piece with each frame showing me wearing a different costume, hat, and earrings, much like those childhood photo strips. Or create a long panel, with each member of the family depicted (including my cats!). Or create a group project and ask everyone to do her own portrait and sew them together in a long, long strip. This format also reminded me a little of the Wanted posters in the post office! Maybe the FBI will hire me to make the 10 Most Wanted Criminals posters in cloth! You never know.

Above are the enlarged quadrants of artist Jane LaFazio's quilted self-portrait (see page 107). She used a strip of images from a photobooth as the inspiration, capturing four different expressions to show her zesty personality.

Using multiple photos of oneself is a wonderful way to show multiple facets of a personality within a self-portrait. It can also be used to chart growth or change. At right is a collection of Jane LaFazio's photo-booth image strips that she and her husband have enjoyed taking throughout the years.

"When I was a kid, my girlfriends and I would spend fifty cents and get strips of photo-booth portraits downtown or at the mall. For each photo, we'd make a goofy face, or change our hair or hat or glasses, become movie stars or punks within those moments as the camera clicked automatically. Four chances to try out a new persona!"
—Jane

capturing a photographic self-portrait

Use these tips to ensure that you are camera ready:

HOLD AND CLICK Hold the camera at arm's length, pointed toward you, and press the shutter—easy with an instant camera, digital, or phone camera, because you can see right away if the shot worked.

TIME OUT Many of the newer cameras come with a timer. Have someone stand in for you in the pose you want and set the camera up to capture it. Press the timer and get into position.

REMOTE CONTROL You can also get a remote device that connects to your camera. Set up the shot, then get into position while holding the shutter release. When you're ready, press it and the camera will shoot.

WORK THE ANGLE Get in front of a mirror and play around with the shooting angles in such a way that you see yourself but not the camera in front of your face. This takes practice.

SHOOT YOURSELF IN THE FOOT Or the hand, or ear, or some other part that isn't your face. It's still you, isn't it?

construction TIPS

RED BACKGROUND I'd recently taken a workshop from Traci Bautista, and loved her tie-dyed paper towel technique. This project was a good chance to use it. Using inexpensive liquid watercolors and following Traci's method, I dyed a bunch of paper towels, shibori style, using red, yellow, and orange watercolor and let them dry completely. I tore (I never cut when I can tear) a piece of muslin 12" × 16" and laid it on my worktable. I cut the dry, brightly colored paper towels in random small squares. Using acrylic liquid matte medium and a foam brush, I glued the small squares onto the 12" × 16" muslin, using the medium both under and on top of the paper. I covered the whole piece of muslin in a vibrant mosaic of shades of red. When it was completely dry (after one night), I used a straight edge, precisely cutting the 12" × 16" sheet into four 8" × 5⅞" pieces. Each piece became a background for each face.

FACES I enlarged the photo strip 400 percent on a photocopier, making each picture 8" × 5⅞", which is the same size that my quilts would be. Using tracing paper, I outlined the head, hair, and facial features. I turned the tracings over to reverse the image, and traced the outline of the head and shoulders onto the paper side of fusible web. I then ironed the fusible web to the back of skin-tone colored fabric. (I used natural-colored muslin.) I cut out the muslin silhouettes and, referring to the original photos for position, I fused the muslin to the paper-towel-covered background, with a Teflon ironing sheet as protection for my iron and ironing board.

DETAILS Going back to the tracings, I outlined the hair portion onto the paper side of fusible webbing and ironed that onto the back of the fabric I chose for the hair. I ironed on the hair in one piece (like a wig), using the tracing paper for correct placement. I used the same technique for the sunglasses, shirt, and for the red lips. The open mouths were a challenge, so I placed a piece of bright white first, then the lips fused onto that. In one picture with the open mouth, I drew the tongue and inside of the mouth using colored pencils right on the white fabric.

SEWING I used my machine, black thread, and a sort of jagged version of free-motion stitching to draw in the hair with thread. I purposely went off the head onto the background with stitching to depict my careless hairstyle. For the shirt neckline, I zigzagged the lines in multicolor thread, and then in free-motion, machine-sewing style, I sewed over the shirt.

I handsewed the lips with red thread, and the sunglasses with gold metallic thread. Using off-white thread, I stitched a line suggesting the nose.

FINISHING I drew the eyes and eyebrows lightly with a pencil on the fabric and then carefully went over the pencil lines with a black permanent fine-tip pen. I auditioned a number of things for earrings (just like in real life) from beads to charms to old earrings and ended up using simple red buttons. I used black fabric as my binding to carry through the photo-booth photo look. The finished size is 33" × 16½".

MATERIALS

Photo-booth photo strip • Muslin • Paper towels • Liquid watercolor paints • Liquid acrylic matte medium • Small foam brush • Black and white fabric scraps • Paper-backed fusible web • Needle and thread or sewing machine • Black permanent pen • Colored pencils

33" w × 16½" h (84 × 42 cm), fabric collage

reflections

SO NOW YOU'VE SEEN THAT a self-portrait can take any form—it doesn't even have to be a likeness of you in any traditional sense. But, as the old song goes, you ain't seen nothin' yet. In this gallery of self-portraits, all created in 2007, several mixed-media artists put themselves on display via fabric, sculpture, metal assemblage, shrines, journals, a medieval mask, an embroidered box of affirmations and wishes, and more.

Each artist describes her or his approach to their work, including a word on technique. But the main purpose of this gallery is to further expand your concept of what a self-portrait can be, giving you more ideas and inspiration for creating your own self-portraits and putting a little bit of yourself in every piece of art you make.

> **"All art is autobiographical; the pearl is the oyster's autobiography."**
>
> — **FREDERICO FELLINI**

self-portrait SHRINE

By Janet Ghio

Creating a shrine to myself was a challenge. It's much easier to create one in honor of someone else. I tried to use elements throughout that reflected who I am and what I believe. I love the vibrant colors and symbols of Mexican folk art; I used those as a starting point for my shrine. The parrot on my shoulder is a tribute to Frida Kahlo. I have a great collection of clothing buttons and also pin-back buttons. The pin-back button that says "Give me all your buttons and nobody will get hurt" actually came from the *Quilting Arts*

booth at International Quilt Festival. This button inspired the use of different kinds of buttons throughout the shrine. They speak to my love of color and embellishment and voice many of my sentiments. Friends and family are important to me. Six little worry dolls dance across my sacred heart. They represent my critique group of six friends. My dog, Sparky, is present and my husband is represented by the letter G. I love my garden and my home and used roses and flowers as a unifying and peaceful element.

The shrine is made up of six pieces (three fronts and three backs). Fabric was fused to a stiff interfacing, then stitched and embellished. One long horizontal hinge joins all the pieces. I laid the back and front center pieces on either side of the "hinge" and stitched all around. Then I did the same with the side pieces.

Materials include hand-dyed and commercial cottons, beads, buttons, charms, and assorted found objects.

9" w × 21"h (23 × 53 cm)
Mixed media with fabric

MEDIEVAL *mask*
By Beryl Taylor

I have a love of all things medieval, and it is a constant theme in my work. The inspiration for my mask came from the Venetian Carnevale, which dates back to 1268. I have always felt greatly inspired by the costumes of that period, and this project gave me the opportunity to make my own mask, which is based on a traditional Bauta mask. This is a full-face mask that is usually identifiable by its stubborn chin line and an abundance of gilding.

I made my mask from papier-mâché using four layers of newspaper and white glue. Once it was dry, I sanded the features smooth. I then painted it with two layers of gesso. When the final coat of gesso was completely dry, I painted it with acrylic paint in a skin tone.

The dark areas around the face are green-colored tissue paper, which is glued to the mask. These areas are embellished with punched flowers of varying sizes painted with Koh-I-Noor paint and gold acrylic paint. The star- and diamond-shaped embellishments were added later. Having added the star and diamond embellishments, I then applied a layer of modeling paste through a stencil in the shape of leaves and swirls. Once it was dry, I painted the shapes with black and gold paint. A further embellishment of squares with beaded centerpieces was applied to the forehead. Sequins and glitter glue were also added to provide a further degree of "gilding."

7"w × 10"h × 3½"d (18 × 25 × 9 cm)
Mixed media

Emphasizing eyelash shapes were cut out and applied to the upper lid, and false eyelashes were applied to both lids.

Although I started the project with a pre-made mask—not one molded to my face—the shape of the face and features match my own quite well. Also, I'm very soft-spoken, therefore portraying my visage as a mask seems to fit, especially as this is a "mute" mask, with no opening at the mouth to speak through. The shapes and colors I chose to decorate the mask reflect many of the symbols and hues I like to use most in my work, thus reflecting me as an artist.

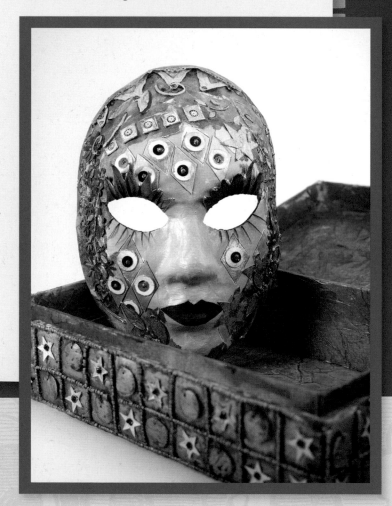

sum of THE PARTS

By K. Wayne Thornley

This piece speaks to the many physiological and emotional layers that come together to make each of us who we are. Physiological elements—skin, tissue, bones—are represented by the multilayered image transfers on the central figure. Emotional layers result from personal experiences, good and bad, and shape our beliefs, our perceptions, and our reactions to the world around us. Our emotional layers are wired into the fiber of our being as deeply as DNA. I often use symbolic imagery to represent emotions, beliefs, personal truths, and secrets. These symbols hover in their respective cages, on the perimeter (I used old colander pieces and wire curled into spirals) but still firmly connected to the physical being.

For this self-portrait, I have used several symbolic images that have been recurring themes in my work over the years. Some are universal, like the cocoon representing evolution or inner growth. Some are very personal and left to the viewer to interpret.

The emerging script is a transfer of my son's handwriting: Latin vocabulary homework. The characters are both beautiful and scarlike, a visual metaphor of the parenthood experience. The encrusted stone pendant represents the weight of the choices and obstacles we face as we make our way through this journey we call life.

Materials include wood, gesso, Liquid Nails, Golden Acrylic Paints, gel medium, matte medium, OmniGel photo transfers, aluminum flashing, hardware cloth, collaged papers, wire, stones, beads, and found objects.

9½" w × 14" h (24 × 36 cm)
Mixed-media assemblage with found objects

SELF-portraits
By Lesley Riley

It is rare to have a photo of oneself that one truly loves, but this one I do. I have been using it as my publicity shot for a few years, so I wanted to approach it differently, use it in a way that wouldn't be so—excuse the pun—in your face. This was accomplished by transferring the photo onto fabric and cutting it into tile-shaped pieces. This created a grid, which was further enhanced with machine stitching (see inset).

The mosaic image on the front is composed of pieces. Since I was creating a journal made of separate pages, I thought that each page would also be a piece of 2008, hence, Pieces of Eight. These pieces combine to make a whole.

To make the journal, I printed "2008" onto fabric, covered each number with mica, and stitched them in place. I attached the self-portrait to a padded canvas board and that became the front cover. Another fabric-covered canvas board became the back cover; I lined both with acid-free, fabric-covered mat board. The journal covers are joined with another piece of fabric for a spine, left wide to accommodate what promises to be a very full book. Luscious handpainted and printed watercolor-paper pages are tied into the book with rayon ribbon, which allows for the addition of more pages as 2008, and my life, unfold.

Materials include ink-jet transfer paper, fabrics, watercolor paper, paint, paintbrush, canvas boards, ribbon, thread, sewing machine, and glue.

11"w × 17"h (28 × 43 cm)
Mixed media with fabric, paper, and paint

TINKERbell
By Ricki Arno

This Tinkerbell, unlike the pixie from Peter Pan, can't seem to get her body off the ground. Her wings can barely flutter, as they are just as fragmented as the words that make up her dress. Her arms are basically useless; her feet are too small and ankles too weak and would be unable to support her body. She has a pretty face, but her mouth is literally filled with flowery words. Her eyes are empty. She carries a bird that needs to be wound up to fly—a chore her hands seem incapable of doing. It is a self-portrait that examines my helpless feelings about events in the world and in my life that I am incapable of fixing, changing, or making better.

20" w × 14.5" h (51 × 37 cm)
Mixed media

BREAKING *free*

By Sylvia Luna / Silver Moon

Breaking Free is my fusion of symbology based on my current life circumstance, one of divorce after being married for more than half my life. This piece was created in the midst of uncertainty, delusion, and apprehension. It is scattered with negative artistic denotations, such as the dead flower. The randomly placed, rusted keys are representative of my sudden inverted security. Despite these major obstacles, I continue to strive toward my new beginning. With a keyhole in place that allows me just a peek into my future, I now have the strength to break free from my past existence and reach up to higher Greatness. In the words of my son, Steve, "You gotta believe, trust, and stand strong." I hope that this art piece gives you strength and inspiration to do the same.

10½" w × 18½" h (27 × 47 cm)
Mixed-media assemblage with found objects

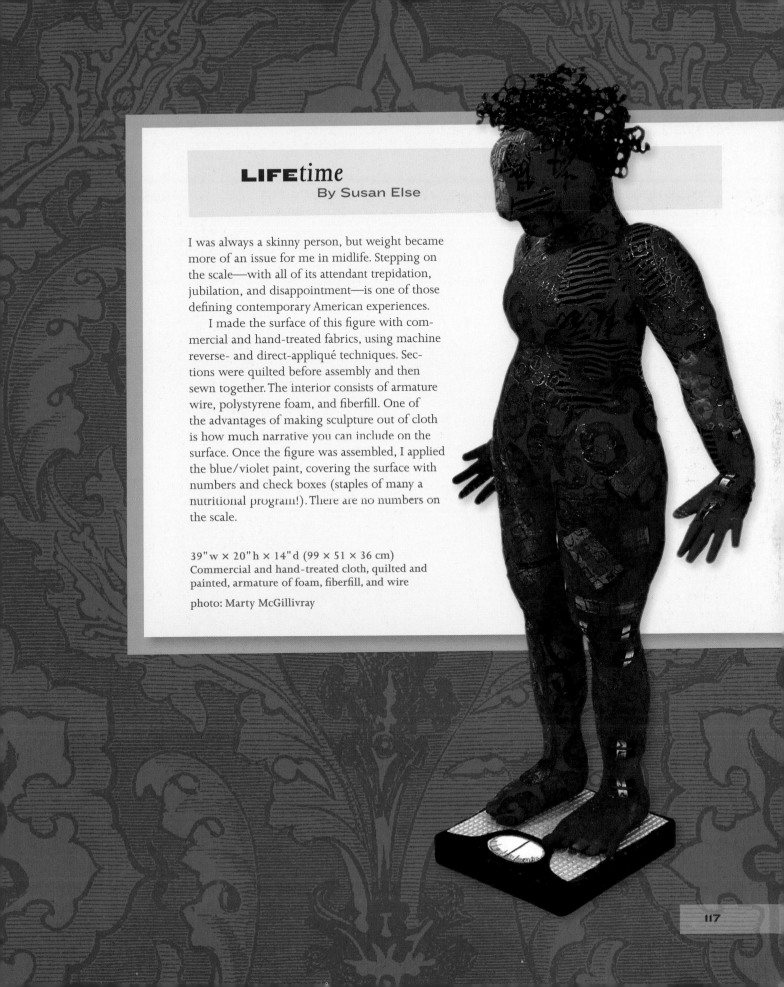

LIFEtime
By Susan Else

I was always a skinny person, but weight became more of an issue for me in midlife. Stepping on the scale—with all of its attendant trepidation, jubilation, and disappointment—is one of those defining contemporary American experiences.

I made the surface of this figure with commercial and hand-treated fabrics, using machine reverse- and direct-appliqué techniques. Sections were quilted before assembly and then sewn together. The interior consists of armature wire, polystyrene foam, and fiberfill. One of the advantages of making sculpture out of cloth is how much narrative you can include on the surface. Once the figure was assembled, I applied the blue/violet paint, covering the surface with numbers and check boxes (staples of many a nutritional program!). There are no numbers on the scale.

39"w × 20"h × 14"d (99 × 51 × 36 cm)
Commercial and hand-treated cloth, quilted and painted, armature of foam, fiberfill, and wire

photo: Marty McGillivray

BOX OF INSPIRATION *for myself*

By Mary Beth Schwartzenberger

I first conceived this piece of art as a box of wishes for my daughter's graduation. I wanted to give her a source of inspiration and affirmations for the wonderful yet challenging years ahead. Then I realized that just as we nurture our children, there are ways we can nurture our creative selves. I created this Box of Inspiration as my reminder to nurture myself and to play. The box combines my love of papers and embroidery. I picked the theme of flowers and butterflies and purposely made it very feminine. I believe symbolism is very important. Butterflies not only represent life's cycles, but beauty and grace as well. From a personal viewpoint, butterflies were always a special symbol between my mother and me. The flowers represent my love of gardening.

I took a plain cardboard box and repapered it with various papers I had altered with stamps. I made an embroidered slip for the box top. I love to garden, so the flower theme worked for me. Just looking at it makes me want to get started. The embroidered cover fabric is douppioni. I wrapped this around a square of mat board, to avoid gluing it directly to the box top. I then glued this wrapped board to the box top. Also, it is a way to reuse the embroidery if the box was ever to be damaged. Then I filled the box with affirmations, wishes, and inspiration.

Materials include a cardboard box, decorative papers, rag mat board, fabric, embroidery floss, beads, and charms.

4"w × 4"h × 2½"d (10 × 10 × 6 cm)
Mixed media with paper and embroidery

Affirmations/Inspirations:

BELIEVE IN YOURSELF

WHAT MAKES YOU HAPPY?

MAKE 10 DECISIONS USING ONLY YOUR INITIALS

BUY A NEW PAINT PRODUCT AND EXPERIMENT

WHO ARE YOU?

EMPOWER YOURSELF

TAKE THE ROAD LESS TRAVELED

COMPLIMENT YOURSELF

RENEW A HOBBY

WATCH THE CLOUDS

HAVE FAITH

COUNT THE STARS

KEEP A SENSE OF WONDER

NEVER QUIT

PAINT YOUR TOENAILS DIFFERENT COLORS

LOOK THEN SEE

ENJOY YOUR GARDEN

IDENTITY and **IF I AM A STRANGER**

BY ELIN WATERSTON

I like to play with images and create digital collages, combining elements that don't quite belong together. This combination is indicative of my personality. I, too, am a combination of qualities that don't quite belong together. While both of these self-portraits incorporate a photograph of me in my "natural" state (tired, up all night, candid), the photo is just one element of the portraits.

In each portrait I included symbols and used processes that reflect aspects of my identity, beyond physical appearance. Blackbirds are a motif I frequently use in my artwork. I'm fascinated with them—not only for their beauty but also for their cultural and mythological significance. The main elements of the digital collage in *identity* are a photo I took in a record store and a direct scan of a Mexican Día de los Muertos skeleton figure.

I don't like to give too much information about my reasons for using specific images; I like the viewer to decide for him- or herself what it means. Let's just say that both portraits show the same me (or side of me): odd, quirky, part vivacious, part dark, and a little inexplicable.

Materials for "identity" (left) include photo and digital collage (of a photo and a scanned object) printed onto white cotton fabric, commercial cotton fabric, and cotton batting.

7"w × 18"h (18 × 46 cm)
Mixed media with paint and fabric

Materials for "If I Am a Stranger" (above right) include photo printed on white cotton fabric, commercial cotton fabric, fabric paint (Dye-na-Flow), and cotton batting.

4"w × 14"h (10 × 36 cm)
Mixed media with paint and fabric

RESOURCES

The National Portrait Gallery

In 2006, the National Portrait Gallery in London mounted a special exhibit titled Self Portrait: Renaissance to Contemporary. The NPG archived online files contain a wealth of information and images related to the self-portrait.

npg.org.uk/live/woselfportrait.asp

Frida Kahlo

There are many books and websites devoted to Frida Kahlo's life and art. One of the best is the PBS archive for *The Life and Times of Frida Kahlo*, a film by Amy Stechler. The Resources page includes a comprehensive list of available research material.

pbs.org/weta/fridakahlo

There is also the 2002 film, *Frida*, starring Selma Hayek and Alfred Molina.

The Self-Portrait Challenge

Here you can participate in the online Self-Portrait Challenge, become an active member of its community, and view past entries.

selfportraitchallenge.net

500 Self-Portraits by Julian Bell

Phaidon Press (2004)

A new version of the original, which was published in 1937, this book takes a comprehensive look at the greatest self-portraits, arranged chronologically, from ancient times to the present.

ArtLex

ArtLex.com offers definitions, information, and images on more than 3,600 art terms, with longer articles on many topics, such as self-portrait.

artlex.com

about the CONTRIBUTORS

RICKI ARNO began her professional career in the 1960s as a fine artist and teacher. She successfully pursued a career in the commercial world of fashion and graphic arts in the 1970s and 1980s, working with Fortune 500 companies in New York City. She then took a surprising detour into confectionary art, sculpting porcelain-quality figurines and decorative details for elaborate wedding cakes. In 2004, she signed a licensing agreement with Schiff Ribbons, becoming their first Showcase Designer. Now, Ricki has returned to fine art. She divides her time between NYC and Jackson Hole, Wyoming, working on her art and maintaining studios in both locations. She teaches collage workshops at the Center for the Arts in Jackson Hole. Please visit the website for more information: www.artassociation.org/classes/workshops.htm#arno. PHOTO BY ANONYMOUS

DONNA ANDERSON is a weaver, photographer, seamstress, mixed-media artist, and painter living in Pennsylvania. She earned her BFA in textile design and BA in graphic design from East Carolina University. She also holds an associate degree in graphic arts. Among her many endeavors, Donna began creating clothes in 2001 and shortly afterward launched OIG, a one-of-a-kind clothing line for little girls. Today, Donna's ambitions lead her painting and mixed media. Donna remains an exercise enthusiast, tree lover, mother of two, devoted wife, and busy volunteer nourishing her creative appetite whenever the opportunity presents itself for her to escape to her studio. Contact her via her website, www.oddisgood.net. PHOTO BY MILES ANDERSON

KATHIE BRIGGS can't remember a time she didn't love fabrics and sewing. In the 1990s, she became intrigued with fiber-art dolls, which gave her a creative challenge coupled with freedom of expression. After living and working for many years in the metropolitan Detroit area, Kathie is finally living her dream as a studio artist in Northern Michigan. While she continues to make art dolls, her current passion is for art quilts since they offer her an infinite range of subject matter. Kathie teaches a variety of fiber arts workshops. More of her work can be seen on www.kathiebriggs.com. PHOTO BY BILL BRIGGS

JULIANA COLES is an artist and creative expression teacher. She received her BFA from the Academy of Art College, San Francisco, and has studied at SMU in Dallas, Columbia College in Chicago, The American Academy of Art in Chicago, and California's New College. She studied with well-known illustrator Barron Storey, who encouraged her mixed-media journals, and with muralist Juana Alicia Montoya, who helped Juliana define her own style of contemporary expressionism. Juliana developed expressive visual journaling as a creative process. Her visual journals are featured in *Making Journals by Hand* by Jason Thompson. She can be reached via the website www.meandpete.com. PHOTO BY JEANNIE MCDOWELL

DEBBI CRANE is a wife, mom, art teacher, art maker, and lifelong resident of Bedford, Indiana. She and her husband, JR, are the parents of two cute and busy daughters, Whitley and Courtney. Debbi holds a BS in education from Indiana University and has taught art to elementary school students since 1995. Debbi has engaged in a yearlong daily art project every year since 2004 without missing a day. Her artwork and articles have been published in books and magazines and exhibited nationally. She coauthored the book *Mixed Mania* (Interweave) with Cheryl Prater. Visit Debbi's blog at www.paperdollpost.blogspot.com. PHOTO BY JAMIE WILLIS

LARISSA DAVIS is art director of *Cloth Paper Scissors* and *Quilting Arts Magazine*. Prior to this she ran her own graphic design company for seven years. In 2003, she and her family relocated from Portland, Maine, to the small town of Hiram near the New Hampshire border. There they enjoy making art of all kinds, raising chickens, renovating their home, gardening, and generally creating lots of cool stuff. PHOTO BY JEFF BAILEY

SUSAN ELSE of Santa Cruz, California, is a fabric sculptor who treats cloth not as a flat surface but as a wild flexible skin for three-dimensional objects. She uses cloth to create an alternate universe, and the resulting work is full of contradictions: It is all at once whimsical, edgy, mundane, surreal, and engaging. Susan's work has appeared in many solo and group exhibitions and selected publications and is featured in three permanent public collections. She can be contacted through her website, www.susanelse.com. PHOTO BY MARTY MCGILLIVRAY

KAREN FRICKE is a resident artist at the Metropolitan Center for the Visual Arts in Rockville, Maryland, where she spends her days playing with all things fiber. See more of her work at www.karenfrickequilts.com. PHOTO BY KAREN FRICKE

JANET GHIO is a contemporary narrative fiber artist who has been making art quilts since 1996. Many of her art quilts and three-dimensional pieces are tributes to the magic and mystery of women. She has written articles for *Quilting Arts Magazine* and has been featured in *Cloth Paper Scissors* and other publications. Her quilt *Autumn Fairy* was selected for the cover of the 2003 *Quilting Arts* calendar. Her work has been shown in many galleries around the country and included in numerous exhibits, including the America From the Heart traveling exhibition and special exhibits at the International Quilt Festival in Houston. Janet lives with her husband and her dog, Sparky, in Kerrville, Texas. Her website is www.quiltcollage.com. PHOTO BY GEORGE DUNN

CHRYSTI HYDECK is an emerging mixed-media artist and instructor who lives in Raleigh, North Carolina, where she also runs her online art supply stores from within her home. Considered an Outsider Artist, she lives with bipolar disorder and Tourette's syndrome. Her work is often very personal, as it expresses her passion for animals, children, and family while also showing her love of whimsy, words, and all things odd. In addition to her art, she enjoys writing and photography. To learn more about her or contact her, please visit her website at www.alteredabbey.com. PHOTO BY JAMES CHANG

CAROL KEMP, aka CarolK, co-owns, teaches, and works at the Art Clinic in Solvang, California. Her art repertoire covers most 2-D media, including assemblage and jewelry, while studies of myth and spirituality fuel her work. In 2006, she completed more than 365 faces, and now she has begun painting portraits of the students at her daughter's school. She is blessed with three kids, a loving husband, yoga, and a passion to create. To contact Carol or see more of her work, visit www.lifsart.com. PHOTO BY RUTH KEMP

KATIE KENDRICK lives with her husband, two dogs, and cat along the banks of the Tahuya River in western Washington. The peaceful beauty of her environment is a constant source of inspiration as is the magical innocence and mystery of her three young grandchildren. She finds art-making to be one of the most powerful ways she can connect with her innermost nature while at the same time discovering her authentic voice. She enjoys the experimental and intuitive layers of creating, exploring the inner and outer worlds simultaneously. Katie teaches workshops nationally. To find out more about her workshops and see her art, visit her blog at www.joyouslybecoming.typepad.com. PHOTO BY KATIE KENDRICK

JANE LAFAZIO is a mixed-media artist who enjoys working in paper and cloth. Jane began teaching her popular Art Quilt Explorations class in 2005 in San Diego, California, and now teaches it online through www.joggles.com. She also teaches mixed-media and watercolor journaling to adults and creative classes for kids. Her artwork has been featured in galleries, juried mixed-media exhibitions, and many publications, including the books *Material Visions: A Gallery of Miniature Art Quilts* and *Fabric Art Gallery* as well as the magazines *Quilting Arts Magazine* and *Cloth Paper Scissors*. Jane also has an instructional DVD titled *The Small Art Quilt*. See more of Jane's artwork at www.PlainJaneStudio.com or follow her creative life at www.JaneVille.blogspot.com. PHOTO BY TIM TADDER

SYLVIA LUNA, aka Silver Moon, has been focusing and developing her art since the death of her only child, Steve, who passed away in his sleep in 1997 without any previous signs of medical problems. She signs all of her artwork "PS. I love Steve!" Sylvia is best known for her Silver Moon Grunge, where she transforms various found objects using a wide array of mediums to appear aged and imperfect. She sells her art and teaches workshops at alternative-art conventions on the West Coast. She recently participated in The Gorey DeTales, a traveling exhibit featuring art and poetry inspired by Edward Gorey. Sylvia is a native of Arizona, currently residing in Gilbert. Visit her website, www.silvermoonstudios.com, and her blog, www.artpubstudios .com. PHOTO BY RON KOUPAL

LORETTA BENEDETTO MARVEL is a mixed-media artist and writer whose work reflects her spiritual connection to family and heritage. Loretta's artwork and writing can be found in her regular column, "The Artist's Journey," in *Cloth Paper Scissors*. She also has been published in *Somerset Studio*, *Legacy*, and in the anthology, *The Circle Continues*. Her artist books and journals will be featured in the upcoming book *True Vision: Authentic Art Journaling* (Quarry Books). When she is not creating art, writing, or entertaining her extended Italian-American family, she also practices law. More of her artwork, photography, and writing can be seen at her blog, www.artjournaler.typepad.com. PHOTO BY JESSICA MARVEL

JENN MASON lives, works, creates, and teaches by the motto "She is able, who thinks she's able." When she's not writing a book, composing a magazine column, designing a product, or teaching workshops, she is either happily telling stories through paint, collage, and assemblage in her Brookline, Massachusetts, studio or spending quality time with her husband and two young girls in their 150-year-old-carriage-house-turned home. She is the author of several books, including *The Art of the Family Tree* (Quarry Books), *The Cardmaker's Workbook* (Quarry Books), and *Altered Paper Jewelry* (Quarry Books). Jenn can be reached through her website at www.jennmason.com. PHOTO BY DEBORAH COSTOLLOE

KAREN MICHEL is a mixed-media artist. She lives in New York where she runs the Creative Art Space for Kids Foundation (www.caskfoundation.org), a nonprofit art center for kids, with her artist husband, Carlo Thertus. Her books, paintings, and collages have been exhibited internationally, and she has been published in various books and magazine,s including her own book, *The Complete Guide to Altered Imagery*. To view more of her work, visit www.karenmichel.com. PHOTO BY KAREN MICHEL

KIMBERLY MONTAGNESE began playing with fabric in the early 1970s. She loved the look of hand appliqué but lacked the patience. Fortunately, a series of mistakes led to her signatire techniques: "no curved piecing," "inside out," and "quilts that keep on giving." Kim has won many awards in Ohio, has displayed her work at the Denver International Airport as well as in private collections across the country, and also has been featured in the *Art Quilt* calender. She is is a member of the Lorain County Piecemakers, Studio Art Quilters Association, and Firelands Association for the Visual Arts, and is proudly associated with Pear Tree Gallery and Ginko Gallery. PHOTO BY GIULIANA MONTAGNESE

KELLI PERKINS is a mixed-media artist and teacher with an insatiable desire to color the world. As a librarian, she shares her love of words and language by frequently incorporating text into her work, inviting you to imagine dialogues layered beneath the surface. In the studio, Kelli manipulates fabric, cloth, ephemera, and found objects into books, dolls, quilts, and whimsy. Her work often appears in *Cloth Paper Scissors* and she loves teaching anyone she meets how to turn common life into art. Kelli lives in Michigan with her three muses, who give her the strength to live her life out loud. Visit her gallery at www.kelliperkins.blogspot .com. PHOTO BY KELLI PERKINS

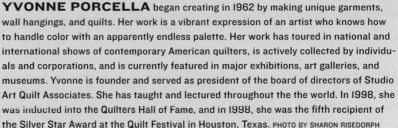

YVONNE PORCELLA began creating in 1962 by making unique garments, wall hangings, and quilts. Her work is a vibrant expression of an artist who knows how to handle color with an apparently endless palette. Her work has toured in national and international shows of contemporary American quilters, is actively collected by individuals and corporations, and is currently featured in major exhibitions, art galleries, and museums. Yvonne is founder and served as president of the board of directors of Studio Art Quilt Associates. She has taught and lectured throughout the the world. In 1998, she was inducted into the Quilters Hall of Fame, and in 1998, she was the fifth recipient of the Silver Star Award at the Quilt Festival in Houston, Texas. PHOTO BY SHARON RISEDORPH

CHERYL PRATER lives in an Atlanta suburb with her husband, Mark, their thirteen-year-old twin boys, Reese and Connor, and her champion dachshund, Trumpet. After many years of acid-free scrapbooking, Cheryl began experimenting with collage and mixed media when her scrapbooks got too fat to close and the format became too restrictive. Cheryl is coauthor of *Mixed Mania* (Interweave) with her friend and fellow *Cloth Paper Scissors* cover artist Debbi Crane. Until someone offers her a TV show making her the Rachel Ray of crafting, Cheryl will continue to work as an executive recruiter, making stuff, writing books, and teaching workshops as time allows. Visit her website at www.zoegraphdesigns.com and her blog at www.praterposte.blogspot.com. PHOTO BY MELISSA FORTENBERY

LESLEY RILEY, best known for her *Fragment* series of small fabric collages, is also an internationally known teacher, quilter, and mixed-media artist with a passion for color and the written word. Her art and articles have appeared in numerous publications and juried shows. As contributing editor of *Cloth Paper Scissors*, Lesley regularly shares her latest ideas and techniques. Through her blog, www.myartheart.blogspot.com, and her website, www.lalasland.com, Lesley aspires to inspire others to find their own voice and share in the magic that is art. When not teaching, writing about, or making art, Lesley, a Washington, D.C., native, loves spending time with her high-school-sweetheart husband, six children, and five granddaughters. Contact her at lrileyart@aol.com. PHOTO BY LESLEY RILEY

KELLY RAE ROBERTS is an artist, social worker, and all-around lover of life and people, who seeks to express a sense of vitality and connectedness in her creations. Having spent most of her life in the company of women, her pieces grow out of the kindred support she has felt from many inspiring women throughout her life. Kelly's work communicates the dreams, struggles, and hopes that she believes are universal among all women. She is unendingly grateful for the spirits of these women who walk with her, in flesh or in paint, on her incredible journey into art, love, and life. Visit her website at www.kellyraeroberts.com. PHOTO BY JOHN SEITZINGER

MARY BETH SCHWARTZENBERGER started creating with fiber in the 1970s. She believes the fiber world is one of the most enthusiastic artistic environments in the arts as artists continue to blur the lines between mediums of paper, paint, and fiber. Mary was trained as a weaver and has evolved into papermaking, collage, and embroidery. Throughout her evolution, fiber remains constant because there is no other tool that produces work with such textural integrity. She lives in Los Angeles with her husband and daughter. PHOTO BY GRACE SCHWARTZENBERGER

TRACY AND ALLISON STILWELL, known as the Artgirlz, are sisters. These two lighthearted women with the artsy outfits and unique haircuts are also seriously talented artists and hard-working businesswomen. When they were young, the six-year age difference was enormous, but later, when both women had grown up, married, had children, and divorced, the bonds changed and grew. They began to collaborate, exhibiting and selling their work. They have always been known for doing unusual, edgy work like goddess dolls and raw-edged quilts, long before either became a trend. Visit their website often to see what's new: www.artgirlz.com. PHOTO BY POKEY BOLTON

BERYL TAYLOR moved to the United States in 2002 from England, having graduated from City and Guilds Creative Embroidery. While in England she spent many years exhibiting her work with a textile group called Threadmill, of which she was a founding member. She also taught many workshops in mixed-media collage. Beryl continues to teach workshops, publish her work in magazines, and exhibit here and abroad. She published her first book in June 2006 with Quilting Arts Publications titled *Mixed-Media Explorations* and has appeared on *Quilting Arts TV*. Contact her through her website, www.beryltaylor.com. PHOTO BY IAN TAYLOR

K. WAYNE THORNLEY explores the alchemy of mixed media in a studio over his garage. Surrounded by bins of old metal objects, wooden boxes, antique photos, salvaged books, paintbrushes, and power tools, Wayne paints, collages, and constructs artwork that explores the common threads of humanity. His work has been exhibited throughout the Southeast and he is represented in several private and corporate collections. Wayne can be reached at urbanrelics@bellsouth.net. PHOTO BY RICK SMOAK

ELIN WATERSTON is an award-winning textile and mixed-media artist and graphic designer, with a BA and an MFA in design. She is the visual arts director, as well as an art instructor, at the Katonah Art Center in Katonah, New York, and an Art*o*mat participating artist. Her work is in many public and private collections and has been exhibited in numerous galleries and museums. PHOTO BY ELIN WATERSON

LINDA EDKINS WYATT discovered textile design while studying at SUNY Oneonta, and after graduating, spent a year at FIT studying commercial textile design. As a print stylist, she won two of the American Printed Fabric Council's Tommy Awards in children's wear. Her textile work has been featured in *Cloth Paper Scissors* and *Quilting Arts Magazine*, the British feminist art journal *n. paradoxa*, and the book *1,000 Artist Journal Pages*. Recently, her art was included in the 2007 Houston Journal Quilt Exhibit. Linda lives in Sag Harbor, New York, with her husband, Hugh, daughter, Amanda, and pooch, Coconut. Contact her at edzellinni@aol.com. PHOTO BY AMANDA K. WYATT

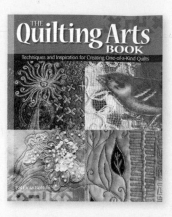